IFRS 15

ISBN: 978-3-9818837-0-1

For more information contact:
Dr. Leo Lehr,
Anni-Albers-Straße 11, 80807 München

Printed in the United States of America

IFRS 15

Revenue from contracts with customers, with SAP Revenue Accounting and Reporting

By Dr. Leo Lehr

Table of contents

List of figures

Disclaimer: The authors of this book are employees of Accenture, but the views represented here are those of the authors alone, and not necessarily Accenture. Accenture and SAP are long-time partners: Accenture works for SAP, implements SAP software for Accenture's own clients, and Accenture purchases SAP software for its own use. Throughout this book, the authors use SAP software as an example for illustrative purposes. However, SAP is one of multiple vendors of revenue accounting software, and Accenture and the authors of this book do not endorse the software of any particular vendor.

Background to this book

In August 2016, I called together some of our company's best experts on IFRS 15 and proposed that we put our heads together. I said, "Let's write a book that makes an implementation of IFRS 15 understandable and accessible for both business as well as IT professionals."

I thought it would be helpful to pay particular attention to the definition of key terms, since understanding these terms is the first step in understanding the scope and the framework of the standard. Furthermore, I wanted our team of authors to focus on a detailed explanation of the five-step approach, which is the guiding principle for revenue recognition within IFRS 15. It was important to me that we do all this in simple language so that even the regulatory material is easy to understand.

In this reference work, we want to point out the complexity of IFRS 15 and make it accessible for your business. Nowadays, businesses must deal with a variety of guidelines on how to report and disclose revenues, based on different accounting standards (e.g. IFRS, US GAAP, HGB/German GAAP). It is our goal to highlight the impact of IFRS 15 on contracting parties, financial statements and external stakeholders. Furthermore, we highlight what will happen during the transition from old accounting standards to IFRS 15, and we show how important it is to prepare for IFRS 15. Implementing IFRS 15 means making changes in business processes and functions, as well as the implementation of new software.

Our goal is to help you implement IFRS 15 in your company by making the intricacies understandable, using SAP Revenue Accounting and Reporting software as an example. We cover this in Chapters 3 + 4 by explaining the process of implementation and migration. Both chapters were written by technical experts who work with SAP RAR every day.

Who are we? The team of authors are experienced management and technology consultants, and we work with revenue accounting and the implementation of IFRS 15 on a daily base. We are an interdisciplinary team with backgrounds in auditing, accounting, software development and implementation. Each of us is highly skilled, and we all come from different industry backgrounds, such as telecommunications, aerospace & defense, platforms & software, as well as high tech. Our combination of skills and deep industry knowledge helps us understand the challenges companies face when implementing IFRS 15. We are experts on what is changing as of January 2018 and how companies should meet their obligations with the right technology implementations.

Who are you, our readers? You are:

- **Managers** who need to implement IFRS 15 and would like to get a general overview on the topic from the regulatory as well technological point of view,
- **Finance experts** who need to implement SAP Revenue Accounting and Reporting within the organization and would like to get a general overview from the technological point of view,
- **IT Specialists** who need to get a better understanding of how IFRS 15 works and how it should be introduced. The book is not relevant for finance experts who want to understand IFRS 15 and its legal and regulatory background in the last detail.

Typically, our readers will be in one of the industries in which IFRS 15 will have a strong impact, such as telecommunications, media, oil & gas, retail, or consumer products.

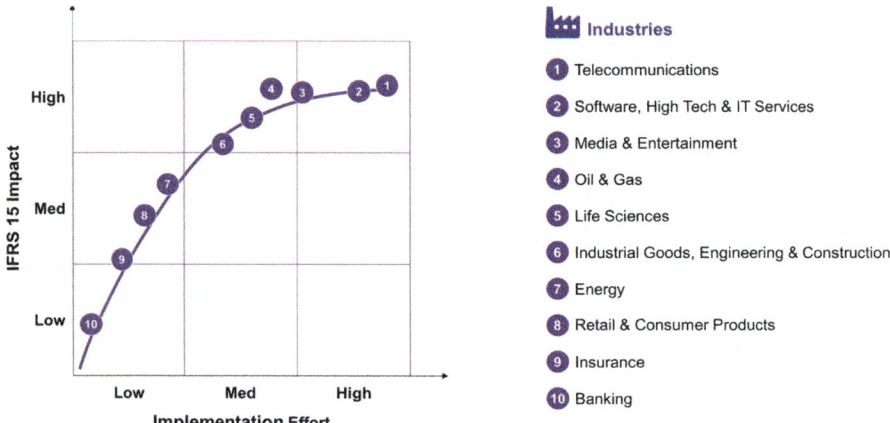

Figure 1   Industries impacted by IFRS 15 and a non-exhaustive analysis of implementation effort

Our book includes an overview of IFRS 15 and, in Chapter 1 takes a look into:

- IFRS 15 as a legal requirement from January 2018 onwards,
- What is new in IFRS 15, who is affected and what does it mean for a company,
- How to recognize revenue in accordance withthe IFRS 15 five-step approach.

Chapter 1 concludes with a case study that illustrates how revenue needs to be recognized with the five-step approach.

Chapter 2 is about how the new revenue standard will impact business operations. It is entitled Cross-functional impact of IFRS 15 – Revenue from contracts with customers.

Chapter 3 explains the technical implementation of SAP's Revenue Accounting and Reporting (SAP RAR) module. Here we:

- Introduce the implementation of the RAR module step by step,
- Provide helpful real-world examples,
- Show dependencies to existing software solutions, such as SAP ERP and SAP Hybris Billing.

Chapter 4 deals with the migration of the data and is packed with useful tips on how to avoid loss of data or data integrity.

In Chapter 5 we summarize our findings and provide an outlook on the future with IFRS 15. We also give you practical advice and recommendations on implementing IFRS 15.

Sincerely,

Dr. Leo Lehr

Legal background – IFRS 15 – Revenue from contracts with customers

This chapter deals with the legal background of IFRS 15 before the technical implementation requirements are explained in the next chapters. We pay particular attention to the definition of key terms which are essential for understanding the scope and the framework. Special attention is given to the five-step approach, which is the guiding principle for an entity's revenue recognition with IFRS 15.

Since this chapter is fundamental, the wording, phrases and quotes are in line with the IFRS 15 standard. To make the content more illustrative, we included some examples from the telecommunications industry.

1.1 Overview: IFRS 15

During the past decades, businesses have become more global and as a result, an international accounting standard was needed. Revenue is an instrument to measure and forecast the financial performance of an entity and is of high interest for a company as well as its stakeholders.

Due to the complex nature of revenue recognition, the standards provided by the International Accounting Standards Board (IASB) and the Financial Accounting Standards Board (FASB), were considered guidance and not defined clearly enough. In addition, the standards left room for lots of interpretation.

Therefore, in May 2014, the IASB and the FASB formed the Transition Resource Group (TRG) to do the following:

- Review the existing accounting standards,
- Identify areas for improvement,
- Remove inconsistencies.

Jointly, they announced the introduction of the International Financial Reporting Standard 15, Revenue from Contracts with Customers (IFRS 15), and introduced a detailed reporting approach for revenue recognition and revenue reporting globally. In the following sections, both institutions, IASB and FASB, are commonly called the "Board".

IFRS 15 covers a set of basic requirements that apply to contracts with customers. The standard consists of an introductory chapter, a main chapter and appendices that cover the definition of key terms, some application guidance and amendments to other standards, among other points.

The introductory chapter contains a short summary of the standard (IN1) followed by paragraphs that provide a high-level overview of the framework for revenue accounting:

- Effective start date (IN2),
- Accounting standards superseded by IFRS 15 (IN3),
- Reason for issuing the new standard (IN4-6),
- Main features (IN7),
- Disclosure requirements (IN8).

With the launch of IFRS 15 and Topic 606, IASB and FASB came up with a standardized approach for revenue accounting (IN9). Both standards agree on basic requirements for revenue recognition and show only minor differences that are not relevant in the context of this book.

The main chapter of IFRS 15 focuses on the objective of the guideline and how to meet the objective. Further, the scope is clearly defined, and detail is provided on recognition and measurement. Overall, the main chapter consists of 129 paragraphs.

IFRS 15 requires companies to provide "useful information to users of financial statements about the nature, amount, timing and uncertainty of revenue and cash flows arising from an entity's contracts with customers", according to the document "IASB 2014. International Financial Reporting Standard 15. Revenue from Contracts with Customers. London: IFRS Foundation Publications Department," which we cite throughout this work.

All customer contracts covered by other IFRS standards are out of scope. According to IFRS 15 paragraph 5, the exceptions are defined as:

a. Lease contracts within the scope of IAS 17 Leases,

b. Insurance contracts within the scope of IFRS 4 Insurance Contracts,

c. Financial instruments and other contractual rights or obligations within the scope of IFRS 9 Financial Instruments, IFRS 10 Consolidated Financial Statements, IFRS 11 Joint Arrangements, IAS 27 Separate Financial Statements and IAS 28 Investments in Associates and Joint Ventures, and

d. Non-monetary exchanges between entities in the same line of business to facilitate sales to customers or potential customers. For example, this standard would not apply to a contract between two oil companies that agree to an exchange of oil to fulfill demand from their customers in different, specified locations on a timely basis.

Considering the exceptions of IFRS 15 paragraph 5, it is possible that contracts adhere to the new standard as well as other accounting standards. In those cases, a detailed analysis of the contract scope is required. It is defined in detail in paragraph 7 of IFRS 15.

Scenario A – If other standards than IFRS 15 specify how to separate and/or initially measure a contract:	Scenario B – If other standards do not specify how to separate and/or initially measure a contract, then:
• An entity shall first apply the separation and/or measurement requirements of those standards	• An entity shall apply this standard to separate and/or initially measure the part (or parts) of the contract
• An entity shall exclude the amount of the part (or parts) of the contract that were initially measured in accordance with other standards from the transaction price, and	
• An entity shall apply IFRS 15 paragraphs 73–86 to allocate the amount of the transaction price that remains (if any) to each performance obligation within the scope of this standard and to any other parts of the contract identified by paragraph 7(b).	

Figure 2   Separation of contracts that fall in the scope of IFRS 15 and potentially other accounting standards

With the establishment of IFRS 15, the following IFRS regulations are superseded:

- IAS 11 – Construction Contracts,
- IAS 18 – Revenue,
- IFRIC 13 – Customer Loyalty Programs,
- IFRIC 15 – Agreements for the Construction of Real Estate,
- IFRIC 18 – Transfers of Assets from Customers,
- SIC-31 – Revenue-Barter Transactions Involving Advertising Services.

Several exceptional standards remain, according to IFRS 15, paragraph 5.

One of the underlying reasons for adopting the new revenue recognition framework is the fact that IFRS and the US Generally Accepted Accounting Principles (US GAAP) report and recognize revenue differently. The effort to harmonize both revenue recognition standards resulted in a five-step approach for comprehensive regulation on recognizing revenue.

The standard explains the main features of IFRS 15: "The core principle of IFRS 15 is that an entity recognizes revenue to depict the transfer of promised goods or services to customers in an amount that reflects the consideration to which the entity expects to be entitled in exchange for those goods or services. An entity recognizes revenue in accordance with that core principle by applying the following steps:

1. Identify the contract(s) with the customer,
2. Identify the performance obligations in the contract,
3. Determine the transaction price,
4. Allocate the transaction price to the performance obligations in the contract,
5. Recognize revenue when (or as) the entity satisfies a performance obligation."

More details follow in Chapter 1.5. To get a clear understanding on what is described within the five-step approach, a closer look at the meaning of the key terms is required.

All definitions are in accordance to IFRS 15, Appendix A, Defined Terms:

Revenue is the amount of money which a business receives for its business activities such as sale of products.

A **contract** is defined as an agreement between two or more parties that creates enforceable rights and obligations, such as setting up a mobile phone contract.

A **customer** is defined as a party that has contracted with an entity to obtain goods and services. The customer would be, for instance, the receiver of the services of the mobile phone contract.

Income is the cash transfer which an entity receives in exchange for providing goods or services or for capital investments.

Transaction price is defined as the amount of consideration to which an entity expects to be entitled in exchange for transferring promised goods or services to a customer, excluding amounts collected on behalf of third parties.

Performance obligation is defined as a promise in a contract with a customer to transfer to the customer either:

- A good or service (or a bundle of goods or services) that is distinct; or
- A series of distinct goods or services that are substantially the same and that have the same pattern of transfer to the customer.

The performance obligation for a mobile phone contract would be the provision of mobile communication services such as the availability of a network and, if provided, the mobile phone.

IFRS 15 provides a standardized approach that makes revenue recognition and reporting more transparent and comparable over industries, capital markets and transactions. Further, it reduces the complexity, as the entities only have to apply one single standard instead of several ones.

For non-listed companies that only have to use German accounting standards based on the commercial code (Handelsgesetzbuch/HGB) and do not account with IFRS, the new IFRS 15 standard is not relevant.

IFRS 15 allows companies early adoption, whereas US GAAP precludes it.

The implementation of IFRS 15 will impact a company's organization in many ways: it influences many business processes and functions; it requires a new technology or a technology update that enables the company to satisfy the requirements of the new IFRS 15 standard; and significant change management efforts are required so that the employees get familiar with new processes and responsibilities.

Outside the organization, IFRS 15 has an impact on the stakeholders of any company due to the new timing or different scope of revenue recognition. Next you will see examples for effects in and outside the organization:

- The approach for how and when revenue is calculated changes. Therefore, financial statements with the new approach are difficult to compare to previous years,

- External investors who invested in a company based on the development of its financial performance over years might face changes when the revenue is recognized and reported differently,

- Shareholders might face a decrease of their yearly dividend,

- Employees who receive a yearly company bonus are affected, since the amount mostly relates to the company's revenues and/or results.

Overall, the introduction of the IFRS 15 standard has a large impact on companies due to the changing revenue recognition procedures and actual timing and amount of revenue to be recognized.

1.2 Impact of IFRS 15

IFRS 15 is a worldwide and cross-industry revenue recognition framework that is binding for companies that prepare their financial statements according to the standards issued by the IASB. "The main principle in the model is that an entity should recognize revenue from contracts with customers that reflects the consideration expected to be received from the transfer of goods and services."[1] Based on the setup, some industries are more affected than others. The following section presents an overview of the telecommunications industry, as this sector is highly affected by the changes coming with IFRS 15. This comes from complex transactions and a contract-based business model with multiple-element arrangements, meaning contracts consisting of more than one product or service.

All of these companies will have to align their revenue recognition to the new compulsory guidelines. In the telecommunications industry, revenue is generated through subscription fees and consumption-based billing of various services – like the use of networks, television or telecommunications. These all need to be considered under IFRS 15.

Besides the service offerings, many companies sell or lease hardware such as mobile phones or modems to make the services available.

When both deliverables are sold together, a combined contract is recommended instead of having separate ones to reflect the business transaction more precisely. Most common are the month-to-month contracts, where the same service is offered on a monthly basis until either entity or the customer cancels the contract.

The telecommunications industry is continually refining its business model and constantly innovating for the advantage of customers. This brings with it new challenges for accounting: especially companies with a focus on wireless equipment will face several changes. In the following section, different working areas are listed that deal with contracts with customers and therefore have an impact on the accounting methods of the entity.

Impact areas:

- In current contracts, customers are often able to modify their contracts easily. For example, a contract can be upgraded even if the contract duration, typically 24 months, has not yet been fulfilled.

---

[1] Jermakowicz, Eva K. Burton Greg F. 2015. *International Financial Reporting Standards: A Framework-Based Perspective*. New York: Routledge. p.468

- A telecommunications provider may offer early upgrade rights, e.g. on mobile devices. Here, it is often the case that the customer receives a material right which needs to be considered as a separate performance obligation.
- For customer retention, companies offer promotions, such as a subsidized mobile device or higher data volume for the same monthly flat price.
- Indirect sales channels, for example selling mobile devices and services via dealers. Entities must consider whether these dealers are treated like principals or agents regarding the sale of mobile devices.
- Contracts lasting longer than one year. Here entities need to evaluate the specific financing component of each contract.

Companies are free to choose whether they implement IFRS 15 retrospectively (i.e. fully restating prior financial statements as if IFRS 15 had always been applied), or as of the effective date with the cumulative impact of the accounting change being presented in equity. All of the impact areas mentioned apply to contracts for private persons as well as for enterprises.

1.3 Shift in effective date

This chapter explains the initial date for adopting IFRS 15 and why the originally planned effective date was postponed by one year. This helps readers understand the complexity of IFRS 15 and why early implementation is recommended.

When the Board announced the new revenue standard IFRS 15 in May 2014, it was initially planned to be effective for all annual periods beginning on or after January 1, 2017. Due to amendments to IFRS 15, the Board decided to postpone the effective date by one year. The new effective date for IFRS 15 is all annual reporting periods starting on or after January 1, 2018. Early adoption of the standard is permitted.

The main reason for the proposed deferral of the effective date was open topics raised by IASB after a discussion with the Transition Resource Group (TRG).

To address open questions, the IASB prepared an exposure draft in which requirements were clarified and illustrated with examples that support the implementation. In addition, the Board received the information from its US stakeholders that additional time for implementation was required. The adaption of IFRS 15 has wide impact on the entire business organization: internal processes and controls need to be adjusted; training for employees is necessary; and software updates or launches are required. IASB said that having one year of additional time reduces the costs of hiring external consultants to help with the implementation of the new standard.

Figure 3   Three dimensions to consider when implementing IFRS 15

The software industry is also highly impacted by the new standard. New regulation causes a high demand for software updates or the development of new IT solutions. In April 2015, when the decision to shift the effective date was being discussed, many IT solutions were not yet available.

1.4 Transition approach

Companies can choose between two different transition approaches when applying IFRS 15: the full retrospective or the modified retrospective approach. The full retrospective approach implies the restatement of comparative periods according to IFRS 15. For this approach, the new standard allows for practical expedients to simplify the restatement. Under the modified retrospective approach, a company does not need to restate the comparative periods according to IFRS 15 but instead calculates the cumulative effect of IFRS 15 to revenues and costs and recognizes the effect in equity. It must also adjust the opening balance sheet when first applying IFRS 15. For a company with a year-end fiscal period, this would be January 1, 2018. This is why this second approach is also called the "cumulative approach".

According to IFRS 15, paragraph C3, the transition approach is defined as follows:

a. Retrospectively to each prior reporting period presented in accordance with IAS 8 Accounting Policies, Changes in Accounting Estimates and Errors, subject to the expedients in paragraph C5, or

b. Retrospectively with the cumulative effect of initially applying this Standard recognized at the date of initial application in accordance with paragraphs C7–C8.

The full retrospective approach implies restatements of all comparative periods shown in the financial statements (quarter and year-end) when first applying IFRS 15. However, this approach also allows for practical expedients to facilitate the transition:

- If a contract was started and completed within the same annual reporting period, for instance starting in January and ending in November of the same year, it does not need to be restated,

- If a contract was completed and included variable considerations, entities may use the transaction price on the contract completion date rather than estimating variable consideration amounts for each prior reporting period,

- For all periods which are available in the financial statement prior to the initial application date, the disclosures of the amount of total consideration allocation to remaining performance obligations and expected timing of their recognition do not need to be included,
- Moreover, the standard allows for expedients regarding contract modifications that have taken place before the beginning of the earliest reporting period presented.

If an entity selects approach b), all amounts that are recognized based on formerly applicable standards remain unchanged, but adjustments due to the cumulative effects of applying the new standard are required.

Considering the differences between the two approaches, we see the following advantages and disadvantages:

Full Retrospective Approach

- + Provides more comparability of financial statements to support the analysis of trends, better understand results, and assist in developing forecasts,
- + Provides practical expedients which ease the transition process into the new regulation,
- − Practical expedients may reduce comparability of financial statements, e.g. trend information may be less understandable or less accurate,
- − Requires a high amount of information to be collected and migrated from the source systems.

Because of required restatements of comparative periods in financial statements, the application of the full retrospective approach will lead to simultaneous reporting for at least one fiscal year. For instance, if a company states one comparative period in its financial statements, it will need to restate all financial statements (yearly and quarterly) of FY 2017 according to IFRS 15 (comparative period) in the financial statements of FY 2018. Ultimately, this company would need to apply dual reporting for FY 2017.

Modified Retrospective Approach

+ Less contracts to be analyzed since only contracts not completed at the initial application date will be adjusted, resulting in lower efforts for migration,

+ Only contracts not completed at the initial application data will be adjusted,

- Does not provide comparability of financial statements,

- According to the IFRS standard additional disclosures are required:

    o Amount by which each financial statement line item is affected in the current year as a result of applying the revenue standard,

    o Qualitative explanation of significant changes between the reported results under the new revenue standard and the previous revenue standards.

In the year in which the entity implements the new standard, revenue will be reported differently than in prior or future reporting periods, causing inconsistent reporting.

Proper documentation of the adjustments is required to make changes traceable and understandable for accountants and other users of the financial statements. At audit time, auditors will take a critical look at the adjustments to verify that the transition was done correctly.

Because a proper transition is critical, it is important that companies define a transition date and clearly communicate this to the entire company, since many processes and business functions are affected.

1.5 Five-step approach

The Five-step approach, which comes directly from the IFRS 15 standard, was already introduced in Chapter 1.1. It provides an overview of how revenue is recognized according to IFRS 15. Within the following sub chapters, each step is explained in detail.

To bridge the gap between theory and practice, we have used an example from the telecommunications industry to explain each step. Furthermore, the chapter concludes with a case study that walks readers

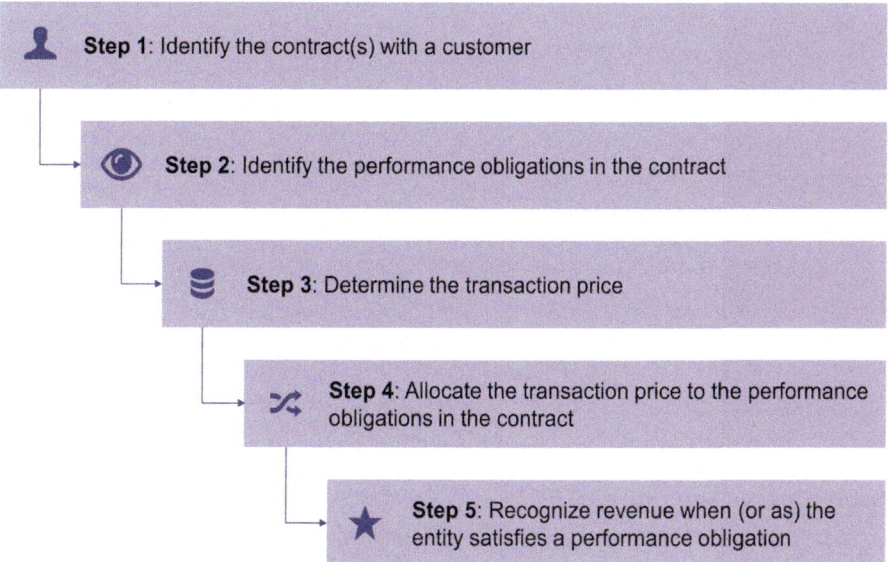

*Figure 4   Five-step approach for revenue recognition according to the IFRS 15
            standard*

through the revenue recognition process and illustrates the process with numbers.

Now, imagine a large telecommunications company. Let's call it TelCom Inc. to keep it simple. TelCom Inc. provides hardware, cable, satellite and Wi-Fi services. Revenue from all of these services will be affected and are part of the following examples.

1.5.1 Step 1: Identify the contract(s) with a customer

A contract is an agreement between two or more parties that creates enforceable rights and obligations.[2]

The following conditions must be met to consider a legally enforceable contract with a customer within the scope of IFRS 15 paragraph 9:

---

[2] IASB. 2014. *International Financial Reporting Standard 15. Revenue from Contracts with Customers.* London: IFRS Foundation Publications Department. p.12. paragraph: 10

- The contract has been approved by the parties to the contract,
- Each party's rights in relation to the goods or services to be transferred can be identified,
- The payment terms for the goods or services to be transferred can be identified,
- The contract has commercial substance, and
- It is probable that the consideration to which the entity is entitled to in exchange for the goods or services will be collected.

If a customer contract does not yet meet all conditions, the entity will continue to reassess the contract to determine whether it subsequently meets the above criteria. From that point, the entity will apply IFRS 15 paragraph 14 to the contract.

Another challenge in this context is contract modifications which play an important role in the telecommunications industry, since customers regularly request changes to their services. Some examples for clarification:

a. A customer increases or decreases data volume,
b. An enterprise needs mobile phones for an additional 50 employees.

According to the new standard, the entity now has to differentiate whether the specific contract modification can still be seen as part of the former contract, or whether it needs to be considered as an entirely new contract.

The following graph shall be a guidance for contract modifications:

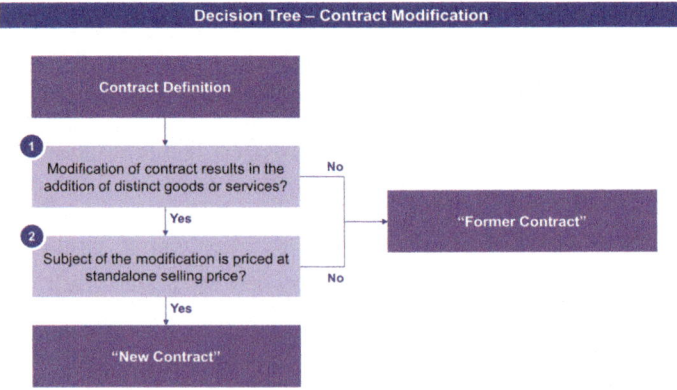

Figure 5   Five-step approach – Step 1: Decision whether the modification of an existing contract results in a new contract

If both questions can be answered with a "yes" by the entity, the modification has to be seen as a new and separate contract.

You'll find further details on contract modifications in the case study.

Step 1: Identify the contract(s) with a customer

 Situation In our example, TelCom Inc. has to state all contracts with each customer separately. Contract modifications are defined as separate contracts under IFRS 15. (Example: An addition of data volume)

 Solution In our example, TelCom Inc. has to check if the following conditions are met:

- The contract has been approved by the parties to the contract;
- Each party's rights in relation to the goods or services to be transferred can be identified;
- The payment terms for the goods or services to be transferred can be identified;
- The contract has commercial substance; and
- It is probable that the consideration to which the entity is entitled, in exchange for the goods or services, will be collected.

If TelCom Inc. has identified contract modifications, these have to be treated as new contracts.

Figure 6   Five-step approach – Step 1: Identify the contract(s) with a customer

1.5.2 Step 2: Identify the separate performance obligations in the contract

A "performance obligation" is the unit of account for revenue recognition. The performance obligations in the contract include promises to transfer goods or services to a customer.

The following conditions must be met to assess the goods or services that have been promised and identified as a performance obligation according to IFRS 15 paragraph 22:

- A good or service (or bundle of goods or services) that is distinct, or
- A series of distinct goods or services that are substantially the same and have the same pattern of transfer to the customer.

A series of distinct goods or services is transferred if the following criteria are met according to IFRS 15 paragraph 23:

- Each distinct good or service in the series that the entity promises to transfer consecutively to the customer would be a performance obligation that is satisfied over time, and
- A single method of measuring progress would be used to measure the entity's progress towards complete satisfaction of the performance obligation to transfer each distinct good or service in the series to the customer. An example for measuring the progress could be the percentage of completion method.

In addition, if both criteria of IFRS 15 paragraph 27 are satisfied, a good or service is distinct:

- The customer can benefit from the goods or services independently or in conjunction with other readily available resources, and
- The entity's promise to transfer the good or service to the customer is separately identifiable from other promises in the contract.

The transfer of goods or services is not separately identifiable if, for example, (IFRS 15 paragraph 29):

- The entity does provide a significant service of integrating the goods or services with other goods or services promised in the contract,
- The goods or services significantly modify or customize other goods or services promised in the contract,
- The goods or services are highly interrelated or highly interdependent with other goods or services promised in the contract,
- Within the context of the telecommunications industry, the precise determination of separate performance obligations plays a crucial role. As already mentioned, a separate performance obligation exists if the customer receives distinct goods and services and can thus benefit from each service individually.

In general, the monthly promise to provide services to the customer reflects the transfer of control where the progress is measured based on the same monthly principle.

Step 2: Identify the performance obligations in the contract

 Situation TelCom Inc. offers one of its customers a bundle of 1,000 call minutes and 1,500 text messages each month for a fixed price. Everything beyond these limits costs the customer extra at a standalone selling price.

 Solution TelCom Inc. will recognize one performance obligation for the flat fee of the bundled service every month. In addition, in each month that the customer exceeds the limit for minutes or messages, revenue will be recognized separately at month end closing.

Figure 7   Five-step approach – Step 2: Identify the performance obligations in the contract

1.5.3 Step 3: Determine the transaction price

The transaction price is the amount which an entity can expect for the exchange of goods and services to a customer, covered in the contract.

When determining the transaction price, the following has to be considered:

1. It has to be identified if the contract includes a significant financing component, that requires an adjustment to reflect the time value of money,

2. An entity must measure the amount of a non-cash consideration in a contract at fair value,

3. A consideration payable to a customer might represent a reduction of the transaction price,

4. An entity must identify if the contract has variable considerations that have to be estimated.

Variable considerations can include discounts, rebates, refunds, price concessions, incentives, performance bonuses or penalties.

If one of these situations exist, the transaction price can be determined by applying one of the following approaches:

- The most probable amount which has the highest chance of realizing considerations will be used as the transaction price ("most likely amount"), or

- The weighted average is calculated to determine the transaction price in what's called the expected value approach.

Step 3: Determine the transaction price

 Situation As part of its discount program, TelCom Inc. offers its customers a contract for 30 euros a month for 24 months, as well as a mobile phone worth 400 euros for 200 euros, if all contractual conditions are met by the customer (e.g. proof of payment).

 Solution As TelCom Inc. knows from market studies in this region, around 50% of all customers will benefit from this discount, and the rest will pay the full price.

Therefore, TelCom Inc. will have to reduce the transaction price of 400 euros for the hardware by the probability-weighted amount of 50% x 200 euros, or 100 euros. This will satisfy the requirements of IFRS 15 with regard to the estimated liability originated by the contract (fair-value approach). This means that TelCom Inc. directly estimates and books the amount of the transaction price which it will receive after the impact of its discount program is taken into account. The whole transaction price for every paying customer needs to be reduced by 100 euros.

The transaction price of the service is not affected by this calculation and is still valid (24 x 30 = 720 euros).

In this situation, when the entity has market knowledge and can predict customer decisions, revenue is affected only by the weighted amount of 100 euros.

	Regular Option	Discounted Option
Mobile Phone Revenue	200 euros (400 x 50% = 200)	100 euros (200 x 50% = 100)
Wireless Service Revenue	720 euros (24 x 30=720)	720 euros (24 x 30=720)
Total Revenue	**920 euros**	**820 euros**

The situation changes if the entity is not able to make predictions about customer decisions. In this case, it would have to deduct directly all rebates offered to the customer, which means revenue would be reduced.

In our example, TelCom Inc. would have to directly reduce revenue by 200 euros due to its discount program, and only 200 euros for the transaction price for the hardware would remain (compared with 300 euros in the example above).

Figure 8   Five-step approach – Step 3: Determine the transaction price[3]

1.5.4 Step 4: Allocate the transaction price to performance obligations within the contract

When a contract has several performance obligations, a business must allocate the transaction price to each performance obligation in proportion to its stand-alone selling price. If the stand-alone selling price cannot be determined by using an observable price, the business will need to estimate the transaction price.

---

[3] PwC. Revenue from contracts with customers The standard is final – A comprehensive look at the new revenue model. https://www.pwc.com/us/en/cfodirect/assets/pdf/in-depth/2014-01-revenue-recognition-comm-supplement.pdf.2014. pp.7-8. [access: 22.06.2016]

To estimate stand-alone selling prices, IFRS 15 suggests several methods that can be used:

- Adjusted market assessment approach,
- Expected cost, plus a margin approach,
- Residual approach (only permissible in limited circumstances).

Discount allocation

Any overall discount compared to the combined stand-alone selling price must be allocated between performance obligations on the basis of a relative stand-alone selling price. In some situations, it may be appropriate to allocate such discounts to some but not all performance obligations.

Advance Payments

If considerations are paid in advance, the business will need to identify if a contract includes significant payment or financing arrangements. If it does, then the contract needs to be adjusted for the time value of money.

Step 4: Allocate the transaction price to the performance obligations in the contract

 Situation TelCom Inc. sells mobile devices and service plans for a monthly flat fee. The monthly fee varies, depending on the choice of the customer. Some customers want to pay a higher monthly fee with no upfront costs, and others want to buy the mobile device for an initial cost and pay lower monthly fees afterwards.

 Solution Even though the total price consumers pay may differ, the transaction price for both performance obligations – e.g. the mobile device and the service plan - needs to be determined based on a specific standalone selling price. In line with IFRS 15, TelCom Inc. will have to recognize the revenue for the mobile device when the customer receives it; likewise, it must recognize the revenue for the service plan over the contract period, no matter when the customer actually pays for the service.

In January 2011, two customers signed up for a two-year contract where the following conditions were given:

	Customer A	Customer B
Mobile Phone	Price: 0 euros (Standalone price is 500 euros)	Price: 250 euros (Standalone price is 700 euros)
Wireless Service	30 euros (monthly)	30 euros (monthly)

According to current practices, revenue would be recognized as follows by most of the telecommunications industry:

	Customer A	Customer B
Mobile Phone Revenue	0 euros	250 euros
Wireless Service Revenue	720 euros (24 x 30=720)	720 euros (24 x 30=720)
Total Revenue	720 euros	970 euros

Figure 9   Five-step approach – Step 4: Allocate the transaction price to the performance obligations in the contract Part 1

There is an advantage when the time range between transfer of the promised goods or services and payment by the customer is expected to be less than 12 months, as no adjustments for the time value of money are necessary (IFRS 15, paragraph 63).

Step 4: Allocate the transaction price to the performance obligations in the contract

Following the new regulations, revenue would be recognized as follows:

	Customer A	Customer B
Mobile Phone	Price: 0 euros (Standalone price is 500 euros)	Price: 250 euros (Standalone price is 700 euros)
Wireless Service	30 euros (monthly)	30 euros (monthly)

	Customer A		Customer B	
Mobile Phone Revenue	295.08 euros	(500/1220) x 720	478.16 euros	(700/1420) x 970
Wireless Service Revenue	424.92 euros	(720/1220) x 720	491.84 euros	(720/1420) x 970
Total Revenue	720 euros		970 euros	

Remark:
The total amount of revenue recognized over 24 months remains unchanged. IFRS 15 implies two major changes:
- Separation of performance obligations (service and product)
- Timing of revenue recognition

Figure 10   Five-step approach – Step 4: Allocate the transaction price to the performance obligations in the contract Part 2

1.5.5 Step 5: Revenue recognition, once performance obligations are fulfilled/satisfied

When it finally comes to the recognition of revenue, entities must align their accounting with the new standard. The starting point will be the identified performance obligations and the allocated transaction prices. The general statement regarding revenue recognition is presented in IFRS 15 as follows:

"...revenue would be recognized when a company satisfies a performance obligation by transferring a promised good or service to a customer, either at a point in time (when) or over time (as) (which is when the customer obtains control of that good or service)."

Control is defined as the ability to direct the use of an asset and obtaining all the remaining benefits from an asset. The benefits of assets can result in cash inflows. To be able to generate cash inflows, assets can be used in following scenarios:

- Use of asset to produce goods or provide services,
- Use of asset to enhance the value of other assets,
- Use of asset to settle liabilities or to reduce expenses,
- Selling or exchanging the asset,
- Promising the asset to secure a loan, and
- Holding the asset.

A performance obligation may be satisfied:

- At a **point in time** (typically for promises to transfer goods to a customer), or
- **Over time** (typically for promises to transfer services to a customer).

A performance obligation is satisfied **over time**, if the following criteria apply:

- The customer simultaneously receives and consumes the benefits provided by the entity's performance as the entity performs,
- The customer controls an asset which is created or enhanced through the performances of the entity, or
- The legal entity does not create an asset for alternative use to the entity but has an enforceable right to payments for performances completed to date.

If a performance obligation was not satisfied over time, then the criteria for performance obligation in "**point in time**" must be applied.

In addition to the criteria for performance obligations satisfied over time, an entity recognizes revenue over time by selecting an appropriate method for measuring the entity's progress toward complete satisfaction of that Performance Obligation.

This section is about revenue allocation when a performance obligation has been satisfied through the exchange of goods and services as agreed in the contract. The IFRS 15 standard provides some methods to measure the progress of the satisfaction of performance obligations. The methods must be applied consistently to similar performance obligations and in similar circumstances. Consistent measurement is important as the revenue amounts need to be remeasured at the end of each reporting period to understand the timely satisfaction of each performance obligation. The entity shall select an appropriate output or input method:

How to measure progress to recognize a Performance Obligation	
Output Methods	**Input Methods**
Functionality Direct measurements of the value to the customer of the goods or services transferred to date, relative to the remaining goods or services promised under the contract.	**Functionality** An entity's efforts or inputs toward the satisfaction of a Performance Obligation (for example, resources consumed, labor hours expended, costs incurred, time elapsed or machine hours used) relative to the total expected inputs.
Good to know Consider the date as the point of measurement. That means what has been delivered by the entity has to be differentiated, e.g. at one certain milestone, from what has been delivered and which goods and services need to be delivered in the future.	**Good to know** If the entity's efforts or inputs are expended evenly throughout the performance period, it may be appropriate for the entity to recognize revenue on a straight-line basis.

Figure 11   Five-step approach – The standard differentiates between output and input methods in order to measure progress to recognize a Performance Obligation

The last step of the five-step approach is recognizing revenue at the right time. The following example for TelCom Inc. may clarify questions about it.

Step 5: Recognize revenue when (or as) the entity satisfies a performance obligation
Situation TelCom Inc receives an order to install telecom equipment in an office building. There are two time slots set up. A two-year service-agreement and an installation time of one year. The entity now has two performance obligations: one for the installation period and the other one for additional services to maintain the equipment.
Solution When the equipment (in this case the mobile phone) is made available, the customer gains physical control over the equipment and TelCom Inc. will determine that the installation was not satisfied at a specific point, but rather over time, as the entity´s performance creates and enhances an asset that the customer controls after creation. Under IFRS 15, entities that provide long-term network services are allowed to defer setup costs, since they are an indivisible part of the ongoing contract. In general, these satisfaction costs, sometimes also called fulfillment costs, will be accounted for with different standards. However, specific circumstances will make these contracts applicable under IFRS 15.

Figure 12   Five-step-approach – Step 5: Recognize revenue when (or as) the entity satisfies a Performance Obligation

1.5.6 Contract costs

Incremental costs which were incurred while obtaining a contract must be recognized as an asset if the entity expects to recover these costs.

It is important to remember that incremental costs are limited to the costs which would have not been incurred if the contract had been successfully obtained by the entity. For these costs, a practical expedient is available which allows the costs to be expensed if the related amortization period is 12 months or less (e.g. sales commissions).

Costs which were incurred to fulfill a contract are recognized, if the following criteria are met:

- Costs are directly related to a contract or specific anticipated contract,
- Costs generate or improve the resources of the entity that will be used in satisfying performance obligations in the future, and
- Costs are expected to be recovered.

Additionally, these include costs such as direct labor, direct materials, and the allocation of overhead that relates directly to the contract.

Assets recognized in respect to the costs to obtain or fulfill a contract are amortized systematically, in line with the pattern of the transfer of goods or services.

1.5.7 Case study

Next, we turn to a case study that illustrates the five-step approach. In the following pages, we present the approach and a corresponding calculation based on a concrete example.

In our example, a customer signed a legally binding contract to buy an Apple iPhone for a stand-alone selling price of 600 euros and a service flat rate for 24 months at a cost of 40 euros per month.

As part of the contract, the customer must pay an upfront fee of 50 euros for the mobile device and the monthly fee of 40 euros for 24 months.

The following example shows a contract case:

Contract

TelCom Inc.

1. Contract Parties	Customer Company
2. Start Date	January 1, 2017
3. Duration	24 months
4. Contract items	• iPhone (32Gb, Wifi+4G, Color: black) – Standalone selling price: 600 euros • 24-month LTE service flat rate – Standalone selling price: 24x40 euros = 960 euros
5. Invoice amount	Upfront fee of 50 euros payable upon contract closure Monthly service fee of 40 euros

17. 4. 17 _Max Mustermann_   17. 4. 17 _Helga Schmitt_

Date and Signature / customer   **Date and Signature / company**

Figure 13   Contract example

Case Study reference data	
Contract Term	24 months
Service Term	24 months
Cash up front (Device)	50 euros
Time unit of supply	Month
Performance Obligation bill amount (for service)	40 euros per month
Device Type	iPhone
Standalone Selling Price – Device	600 euros
Standalone Selling Price - Service	960 euros

Figure 14   Case Study reference data

* * *

In the first step, we have to identify the contract. According to Chapter 1.5 we see:

- The contract has been approved by both parties,
- The contract has commercial substance,

- What the customer gets (mobile phone and service flat) and what the entity gets (money) is identifiable,
- The payment terms are stated (upfront fee of 50 euros for the iPhone and a monthly fee of 40 euros),
- The collection of the payments is probable,
- Conclusion from the points above: A contract with a customer exists.

* * *

In the second step, we identify the performance obligations of the contract. From Chapter 1.5 we remember that performance obligations in a contract include promises to transfer goods or services to a customer.

Identify Performance Obligations	
Contract Term	24 months
Service Term	24 months
Cash up front (Device)	50 euros
Time unit of supply	Month
Performance obligation bill amount (for service)	40 euros per month
Device Type	iPhone
Standalone Selling Price – Device	600 euros
Standalone Selling Price - Service	960 euros

Figure 15   Case study – Identify Performance Obligations

In our case, we identified two Performance Obligations:

- Service (flatrate),
- Device (iPhone).

* * *

In step three, the transaction price has to be determined. When determining the transaction price, the company also needs to take into account significant financing components. What's important here is that the cash selling price that would have been obtained is used as the basis for the revenue to be recognized (instead of a different price linked to the customer's credit worthiness).

Determine transaction price (based on cash to be received)	
Contract Term	24 months
Cash up front	50 euros
Service Contract price	960 euros
Total transaction price	1,010 euros

Figure 16   Case study – Determine transaction price

Variable considerations can include discounts, rebates, refunds, price concessions, incentives, performance bonuses or penalties:

Figure 17   Case study – Variable considerations with impact on the transaction price

In our example, the transaction price consists of a single upfront payment of 50 euros, plus the monthly contract fee of 40 euros. Since the contract term is defined for 24 months, the service contract price is 960 euros (24 x 40 euros = 960 euros). No variable considerations exist in this case.

Summing up both items, our transaction price can be determined to be 1,010 euros.

* * *

The fourth step is to determine the correct allocation of the transaction price to the performance obligations. In our example, the stand-alone selling price of the two performance obligations of the contract has already been defined. It was a price of 600 euros for the device and 960 euros for the service.

Now the allocation factor needs to be calculated. This is done to determine how much of the transaction price will be allocated to the device and to the service, since the stand-alone selling prices of both performance obligations differs from the total transaction price the entity is going to receive.

The combined stand-alone selling price of both performance obligations is 1,560 euros; the sum of the transaction price of both performance obligations is 1,010 euros.

The allocation factor is the percentage of each performance obligation, based on the stand-alone selling price. In our example, this means:

- 600 euros/1,560 euros = 38.46 % for the device
- 960 euros/1,560 euros = 62.54 % for the service

Now the percentages have to be multiplied by the transaction price of 1,010 euros to calculate the amounts for both performance obligations which can later be booked in the financial statement.

- 1,010 euros x 38.46% = 388.45 euros
- 1,010 euros x 62.54% = 621.55 euros

Allocation of transaction price		Remark
Contract term	24 months	
Device standalone selling price	600 euros	
Service standalone selling Pprice	960 euros	
Total standalone selling Price	1,560 euros	
Device allocation factor	38%	= 600 / 1,560
Service allocation factor	62%	= 960 / 1,560
In total	100%	
Total transaction price	1,010 euros	See Fig. 16
Performance obligation total revenue (device)	38% = 388.45 euros	= 38% * 1,010 euros
Performance obligation total revenue (service)	62% = 621.55 euros	= 62% * 1,010 euros
Performance obligation unit allocation service	25.90 euros per month	= 621.55 euros / 24 months

Figure 18   Case study – Allocation of transaction price

* * *

In the final step, we recognize the revenue. With the data that has been calculated already, we can identify how much the entity is able to book in each period.

According to IFRS 15, the entity is allowed to book the whole amount of the device (388.45 euros) directly in the first period. The amount of the service needs to be equally divided by 24 months over the total contract period. The calculation, therefore, is 621.55 euros/24 month = 25.90 euros/month.

As shown in the following table, the amount of the device and 1/24 of the total service fee can be booked in the first period (where every period T symbolizes one single month), thus 388.45 euros + 25.90 euros = 414.35 euros. From period T2 until period T24 (each a period with a length of 1 month), the revenue amount to be recognized is 25.90 euros.

Financial Statement (values in euros)		Total	T1	T2	T3	...	T24
Profit & Loss	Device revenue	388.45	388.45	-	-	-	-
	Service revenue	621.55	25.90	25.90	25.90	25.90	25.90
	Total revenue	1,010.00	414.35	25.90	25.90	25.90	25.90

Figure 19   Case study – Financial statement

Conclusion

In the previous pages, we have shown the five steps to follow when applying IFRS 15, based on an example from the telecommunications industry. The example stated all areas that need a special focus and gave tips to guide you through the five-step approach.

1.6 Impact on the financial statement

A contract between an entity and a customer influences the entity's financial statement. Depending on the *payment* for goods and services and the *transfer* of goods and services to the client, the type of financial posting differs.

The presentation of the performance of a contract in financial statements is a crucial part of the new IFRS 15 regulation.

According to the regulation, the performance of a contract shall be presented as:

1. **Contract Asset:** A contract asset is an entity's right to consideration, in exchange for goods or services that the entity has transferred to a customer when that right is conditional on something other than the passage of time.[4]
2. **Contract Liability:** A contract liability is an entity's obligation to transfer goods or services to a customer for which the entity has received consideration (or an amount of consideration is due) from the customer.[5]
3. Receivables are unconditional rights to consideration. Receivables cannot be netted against contract liabilities.

Depending on whether either party has performed, i.e. if the entity has satisfied its performance obligations, whereas the customer has not, a contract asset is recognized. The customer performs by making the payment to the entity. If this is done before the entity provides its obligation, e.g. by transferring goods and services to the customer, a contract liability has to be presented on the financial statement.

For the first item – contract asset – the payment is not requested before the entity transfers goods or services to the customer, which means that the revenue is unbilled.

For the second item, a contract liability is booked to the financial statement when a customer pays consideration before the performance obligation is satisfied e.g. goods and services have been transferred. The revenue in this case is deferred, e.g. it is a liability.

IFRS 15 mentions quantitative and qualitative disclosure requirements where entities are required to disclose more information about contracts with customers than so far required through IAS 18 and IAS 11.

---

[4] IASB. 2014. *IFRS 15 Revenue from Contracts with Customers*. London: IFRS Foundation Publications Department. p. 33. paragraphs: 105-109
[5] IASB. 2014. *IFRS 15 Revenue from Contracts with Customers*. London: IFRS Foundation Publications Department. p. 33. Paragraphs: 105-109

The main objective of the disclosure requirements is to provide detailed information about the nature, amount, timing and uncertainty of revenue and cash flows in the financial statements. This provides users of financial statements sufficient information about contracts with customers and insights into the entity's performance.

IFRS 15 includes the following disclosure requirements:

- Disaggregation of revenue,
- Contract balances,
- Performance obligations,
- Costs recognized to obtain or fulfill a contract,
- Significant judgements.

Disaggregation of revenue

According to IFRS 15, revenues from contracts with customers shall be disaggregated. How much detail is disclosed depends on the specific circumstances of each entity. Some entities may determine that a disaggregation of revenue shall be adequate using existing segments and timing of the transfer of goods or services (point in time vs over time). However, this might not be sufficient or appropriate for other entities.

Additional categories as a basis for disaggregation of revenue include:

- Type of good or service,
- Geographical regions,
- Market or type of customer,
- Type of contract,
- Contract duration,
- Sales channels.

While choosing categories for the disaggregation of revenue, entities shall consider how revenue is presented for other purposes, such as annual reports or investor presentations.

Entities must disclose sufficient information for stakeholders for them to be able to understand the connection between disaggregated revenue and revenue information that is disclosed for each reportable segment.

Detailed disclosure requirements

Paragraph in IFRS 15	Disclosure requirements	Revenue recognized		Is it new in IFRS 15?
		Over time	At a point in time	
116-118	**Contract balances**			
	Opening and closing balances (Contract with customers) for: - Contract assets - Contract liabilities - Receivables from contracts with customers	👍	👍	Partial
	Opening and closing balances of receivables, contract assets and contract liabilities.	👍	👍	Existing
	Revenue recognized from the period that was part of the contract liability balance.	👍	👍	Existing
	Use qualitative information to explain the relationship between the specific timing of payments and the typical timing.	👍	👍	Existing
	Changes in the contract asset and contract liability assets need to be explained. Examples of changes include:	👍	👍	Existing
	a) In business combinations	N/A	N/A	New
	b) Catch-up adjustments in revenue that change the contract asset or contract liability, e.g. change in the measure of progress or in the estimate of the transaction price or a contract modification	N/A	N/A	Existing
	c) Weakening of a contract asset	N/A	N/A	Existing
	d) Time changes for a right to a consideration to become unconditional	N/A	N/A	Existing
	e) Time changes for a Performance Obligation to be satisfied	N/A	N/A	Existing
119-122	**Performance Obligations**			
	Information about performance obligations in contracts with customers have to include:	👍	👍	N/A
	a) Typical satisfaction date, including bill-and-hold arrangements	👍	👍	New
	b) Significant payment terms, e.g. financing component included	👍	👍	Existing
	c) What kind of deliverables are there?	👍	👍	Partial
119-122	**Performance obligations**			
	d) Obligations for returns, refunds and other similar obligations	N/A	N/A	New
	e) Types of warranties and related obligations	N/A	N/A	Partial
	Information needed on Performance Obligations a) Sum of the transaction price	N/A	N/A	Existing
	b) Date of recognition as revenue aligned with paragraph 120 in either of the 2 ways: I. Quantitative basis, using expected remaining duration of the performance obligation. II. Qualitative basis	👍	👍	Existing
	No disclosure information from §120 needed, if: a) Performance Obligation lasts less than a year b) Revenue is recognized aligned with paragraph	N/A	N/A	N/A
	Qualitative explanation, why the practical expedient in paragraph 121 is applied, and whether further consideration is not included in the transaction price and thus not part of the disclosure information.	👍	👍	Existing

Paragraph in IFRS 15	Disclosure requirements	Revenue recognized		Is it new in IFRS 15?
		Over time	At a point in time	
123-126	Significant judgements in the application of this standard			
	Anything that has to do with judgements shall be disclosed, especially: a) When Performance Obligations are satisfied b) Transaction price	👍	👍	Partial
	For Performance Obligations satisfied over time, the two following points shall be disclosed:	👍	N/A	N/A
	a) Description of output and input methods used to recognize revenue	N/A	N/A	New
	b) Why are these methods used?	N/A	N/A	Existing
	When Performance Obligations are made at a point in time, an entity needs to describe when a customer receives a good or service.	N/A	👍	Partial
	Methods, inputs and assumptions need to be described as follows: a) Determine transaction price b) Is the consideration variable? c) Allocate the transaction price d) Measure obligations for returns, refunds and other similar obligations	👍	👍	Existing
127-128	Assets recognized from the costs to obtain or fulfil a contract with a customer			
	Entity needs to state: a) A judgement about the amount of the costs b) Description of the method to determine the amortization rate	👍	👍	Existing
	Entity needs to disclose: a) Closing balances of assets by main category of asset b) Amount of amortization and impairment losses during the period	👍	👍	Existing

Figure 20   Disclosure requirements table

1.7 Revenue recognition and audits

Revenue recognition highly influences the financial statements of a company. Under IFRS 15, the revenue of a company in one country becomes comparable to revenue of the same company but in another country.

A company's adherence to the compliance process is generally monitored on four different stages:

1. Internal controls, e.g. rules and processes,
2. Internal audit,
3. External audit,
4. National or international authorities.

To monitor compliance with IFRS or US GAAP, most companies establish internal control systems to ensure that the standards are applied. Nearly all companies of certain size have an internal audit department that monitors adherence to compliance processes on a regular basis. Furthermore, many are involved in setting up controls for their business processes so that compliance is part of day-to-day operations.

Another way to monitor compliance is with an external audit that is done by an independent auditing company. It is compulsory for almost all companies to engage an external auditor to audit financial statements. An external audit includes the audit of IT systems which are relevant for financial reporting. In addition, an external auditor might be engaged to perform special reviews.

When adopting IFRS 15, companies must adjust their internal controls and should align with their external auditors as early as possible about the new regulations. These adjustments relate to business processes and functions, as well as to the company's accounting software.

IFRS 15 superseded six former accounting standards and interpretations, hence it is critical that the new standard works properly from the first day of implementation. In addition, open contracts need to be modified to comply with IFRS 15. For both points, companies need a working and stable software solution in place that can help manage the changes. To avoid any mismatches, manipulation or fraud, it is best to account for revenue using the old and new standards simultaneously for a couple of interim reporting periods.

Since the impact on the financial statements is significant, it is even more important that companies plan the adoption of IFRS 15 as early as possible and align every step with their internal audit department as well as external audit company.

Cross-functional impact of IFRS 15 – Revenue from contracts with customers

2

In this chapter, we will outline the possible cross-functional impact of IFRS 15 on an organization. We will provide an overview of how companies may be affected by the implementation of the new standard and present a detailed explanation of the impact on 10 key cross-functional areas. Finally, we will explain risks and challenges to companies before and during IFRS 15 implementation and how they can deal with these.

James Schnurr, who served as the chief accountant of the U.S. Securities and Exchange Commission (SEC) from October 2014 until November 2016, described in a speech published on the SEC's website the needs of companies to plan appropriately for IFRS 15 implementation:

"Implementation of the new standard requires significant effort by companies, including analyzing contracts and designing new systems, processes and controls. Given the importance of high quality application of the standard, I believe executive management, the audit committee, and the company's external auditor should discuss implementation status and plans, as well as the allocation of sufficient resources with appropriate skillsets to execute the plan."

Schnurr's comments summarizes very well the most important aspects to consider when companies prepare for IFRS 15 adoption.

2.1 IFRS 15 is more than an accounting change

The application of the IFRS 15 accounting standard is more than an accounting change, and it will likely impact all processes related to revenue recognition in your organization.

The impact will depend on your company's offerings, type, and number of contracts, as well as bundle of services and products provided. Companies may need to make changes in their organization, processes and technology to enable compliance with the new regulation.

Several company areas will be affected:

- **Revenue-related process areas** will be impacted – including planning, procurement, supply chain, billing, customer management, contracting, risk management and legal.
- New revenue recognition processes enabled by technology will impact the **organization and talent**. Change management will be required.
- Systems in the area of CRM, billing, contract management, order-management, planning, consolidation, and reporting will be impacted as IFRS 15 is integrated into a **complex technology landscape**. This requires identification of additional data and analytics, as well as collection, cleansing and storage from source systems.

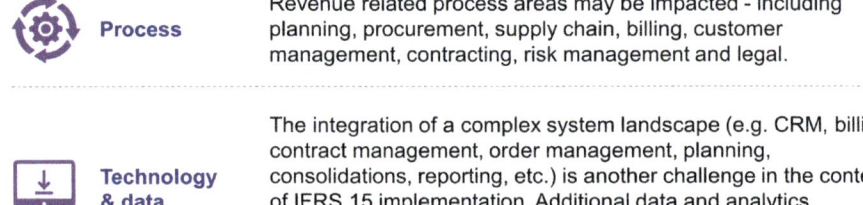 **Process** — Revenue related process areas may be impacted - including planning, procurement, supply chain, billing, customer management, contracting, risk management and legal.

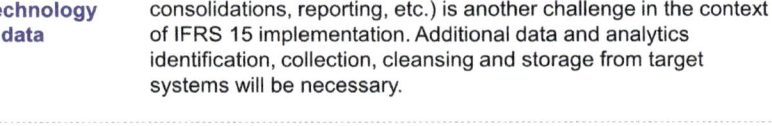 **Technology & data** — The integration of a complex system landscape (e.g. CRM, billing, contract management, order management, planning, consolidations, reporting, etc.) is another challenge in the context of IFRS 15 implementation. Additional data and analytics identification, collection, cleansing and storage from target systems will be necessary.

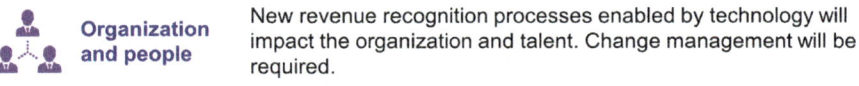 **Organization and people** — New revenue recognition processes enabled by technology will impact the organization and talent. Change management will be required.

Figure 21   Areas affected by IFRS 15

IFRS 15 is an accounting standard that applies to all contracts with customers to provide goods and services in the ordinary course of business. Therefore, the new standard has a wide, cross-functional reach and impact. Companies will need to carefully apply the standard for all contracts, considering the specific terms and context, including implied contract terms. In addition, companies must apply the requirements of IFRS 15 consistently to all contracts with similar characteristics and similar circumstances.

In some cases, companies must make estimates and judgments. When this is necessary, the organization should not only gather more data and information to recognize and disclose revenues, but it should also justify the judgments that were applied when making estimates.

Our experience shows that with IFRS 15 comes the need to review revenue accounting processes for significant activities, and this can take much longer than expected. During this process, we recommend that the CFO consult with the company's auditors as well as the FASB, IASB and the SEC.

The new accounting standard might also make it necessary to review company contract management procedures and solutions. You may need to consider points like: Do we already have a process and a technical solution in place that enables us to judge all possible contract considerations? Are we tracking all relevant contract events and contract modifications? Is our IT landscape capable of capturing all relevant information for revenue recognition?

Although most of these points will be seen as challenges, we do suggest looking at them as opportunities as well. The review of processes is indeed a chance to improve them.

2.1.1 How processes are impacted: End-to-end processes

Your organization's end-to-end processes will be impacted by the new regulation. This includes: order to cash, revenue accounting, and record to report.

In the next figure, Figure 22 you will see more than 20 processes potentially impacted by IFRS 15, from the management of a sales order to the recognition of revenues, the fulfillment of a product and the related invoicing/billing. All of these processes have to be considered and potentially revisited during the design of your IFRS 15 implementation.

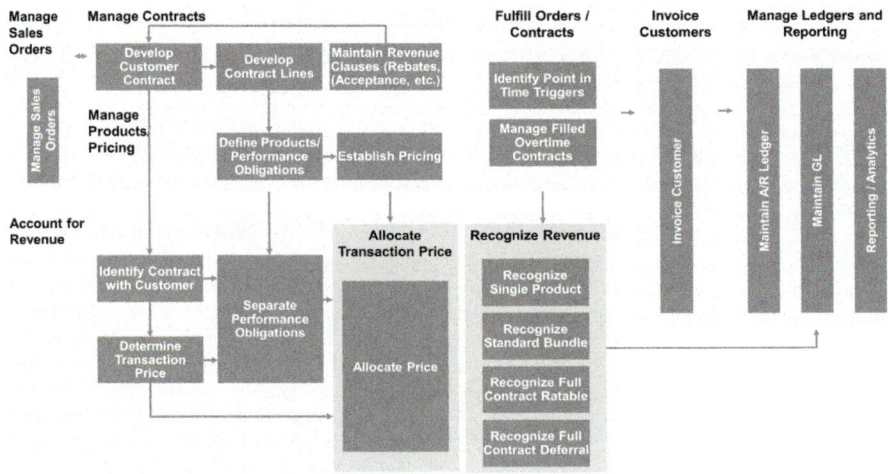

Figure 22   Overview of processes potentially impacted by IFRS 15

2.1.2 Impact on the organization: Compliance and communication

Adopting a new standard is also a chance to improve on the organizational structure as well.

Here are three places that can be evaluated for further improvement as you prepare for IFRS 15:

Functional stewardship

- Create a revenue operations team responsible for executing all finance-related revenue process work
- Consider shared services or outsourcing arrangements as part of a single global team strategy

Talent management/ training

- Evaluate existing capabilities to support changing regulatory requirements and assess the need to acquire talent versus training existing staff
- Develop a structured training program to keep staff informed

Roles and responsibilities

- Define roles and responsibilities for the entire revenue management cycle across all functions involved

Figure 23   Overview of organizational measures to prepare for IFRS 15

2.1.3 Impact on technology and data: Choosing the right accounting solution

One of the key assessments and decisions your organization will have to make is which solution to use for revenue recognition.

Since out-of-the-box technology solutions are rare, we recommend using one of three approaches, depending on your company's size, transaction volumes, products and customer contracts:

1. **Accounting solution in your ERP**: In this approach, the objective is to implement IFRS as much as possible within existing ERP systems. This typically implies manual efforts (with some minor degree of automation, e.g. Excel macros). The approach is recommended for small companies with small transaction volumes and highly standardized products and customer contracts.

2. **Accounting solution via cloud or on premise bolt-on**: With this approach, revenue accounting processes are "externalized" with a bolt-on. Here specific attention must be paid to the integration and interfaces. Most standard solutions provide several integration scenarios which must be carefully evaluated. Typically, bolt-ons are implemented at medium to large companies with high transaction volumes and a differentiated product portfolio or individualized customer contracts.

3. **Custom accounting solution**: While this option gives you maximum flexibility and allows you to realize specific requirements, it is

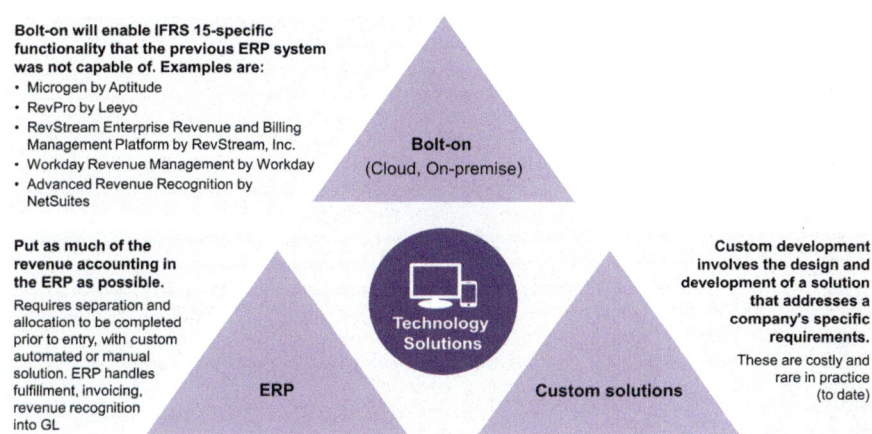

Figure 24   Overview of possible technical solutions

unfavorable in terms of total cost of ownership. Especially due to high maintenance costs, this option is rarely used.

For bolt-ons, companies can choose from several solutions in the market which all have advantages and disadvantages. Two major players are Aptitude Revenue Recognition Engine and SAP Revenue Accounting and Reporting (SAP RAR).

Aptitude is a leading provider of software for full IFRS 15 compliance. It is a made-to-order solution for IFRS 15, and in the United States, three out of the four largest telecommunications operators have chosen Aptitude Revenue Recognition Engine (ARRE). No bespoke coding of additional rules or recognition patterns are required within the IFRS 15 engine to meet requirements. Aptitude has a track record of helping telecommunications companies meet the requirements of IFRS 15, and it has processed more than 300 scenarios from more than 40 of the world's leading operators.

SAP RAR is a revenue recognition solution from one of the largest providers of ERP software. SAP's RAR 1.2 version, released in June 2016, integrates the

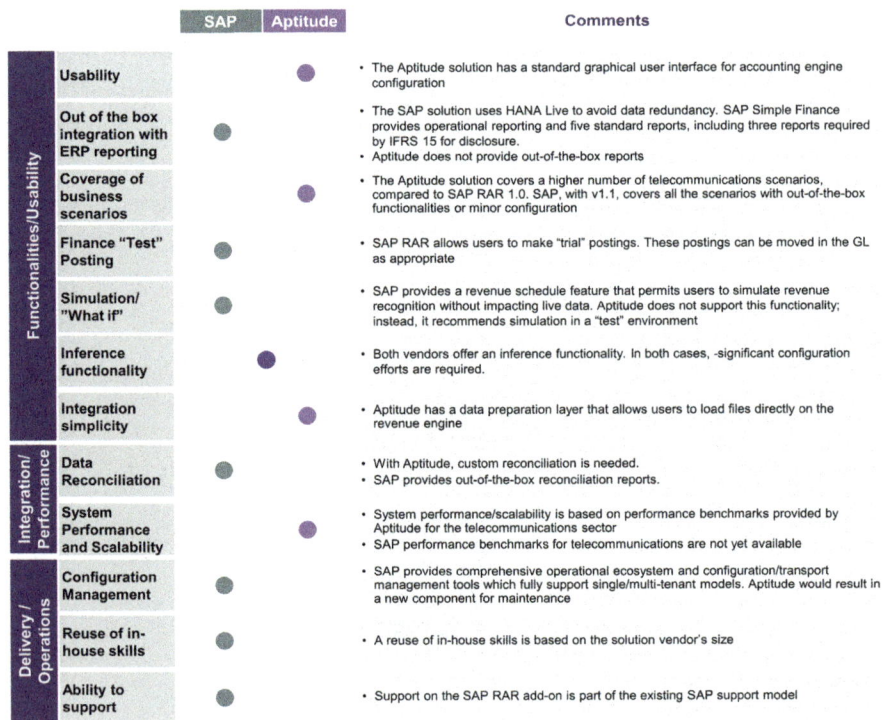

Figure 25   High-level comparison of SAP RAR and Aptitude Revenue Recognition Engine

accounting software with both SAP solutions and non-SAP systems, using SAP's adapter framework. Those companies using a SAP platform strategy, and those that have multiple SAP systems in place often choose SAP RAR. It is a generic, open-ended product which limits the amount of customization and configuration needed, depending on the company's requirements. SAP also offers 24-hour support.

Remember to plan enough time to select your IFRS 15 accounting solution. If you are considering SAP RAR, you'll find further information about it in Chapter 3.

2.2 Assessing the 10 key cross-functional areas impacted by IFRS 15

We see 10 areas that will be impacted by the adoption of IFRS 15. These include:

- Enterprise risk and controls
- Business operations
- Industry specific issues
- Tax accounting and methods
- Public relations and communications

- Remuneration schemes
- Management information
- IT systems
- Processes
- Change management

Figure 26   10 key areas of cross-functional impacts

2.2.1 Enterprise risk and controls

As part of rolling out the new revenue recognition standard, revenue controls and risks should be reviewed.

Internal controls for revenue accounting should also be applied to all risks that relate to present fair revenue for the reporting period. This means internal controls should be designed specifically for particular risks:

- **Occurrence and existence** – Were sales of products or services made to valid customers, and do they meet the criteria for valid sales? Are only those revenues applicable to the reporting period presented in the financial statements?
- **Completeness** – Have all revenues of the entity been reflected in the financial statements?
- **Valuation and accuracy** – Are sales or other revenues valued properly? That is, do they reflect arms-length valuation for products, services, or transactions recorded during the reporting period?
- **Cut-off** – Has the revenue actually occurred in the reporting period presented?
- **Classification and disclosure** – Are the revenues presented in the proper account classifications, and are all necessary disclosures included?

In addition, companies must address how processes will change, based on what is needed by compliance and internal auditors.

Furthermore, IFRS 15 might have an impact on your company's accounting manuals and chart of accounts.

- **Accounting manuals** should be updated to cover all new IFRS 15 reporting requirements.
- Due to different reporting requirements for the legal entity **(local reporting)** and the group **(IFRS group reporting)**, the chart of accounts in the accounting software potentially needs to be updated.

Key matters to think about regarding Enterprise Risk and Control:

- Organizations should assess how their internal controls are impacted, as well as risks related to those controls, due to the implementation of IFRS 15.

- Companies should consider whether they need to review their risks and controls linked to the accounting manuals and changes in the chart of accounts.

2.2.2 Industry-specific issues

IFRS 15 is a challenge for many companies. Let's look at the case of telecommunications companies, which will be significantly impacted by the new standard due to frequent modifications by customers to their subscription plans, as well as continued subsidies for bundled offerings for devices and services.

The relative stand-alone selling price **allocation could differ** for each combination of handset and service plan, depending on the size of the discount provided on the handset and the expected revenue from future services.

- Therefore, telecommunications companies will likely need to update their accounting and information systems to track individual transactions and allocate considerations appropriately.
- Grouping similar contracts in portfolios and accounting for them together is allowed under IFRS 15.

An overview of the change aspects at telecommunication companies is given in Figure 27:

The change aspects	Impact on ...				
	timing	reporting	revenue	expenses	Profit/tax/equity/cash flow
❶ Identify unique Performance Obligations	✕	✓	⬆⬇	⬆⬇	⬆⬇
❷ Significant financing component	✓	✓	⬆	✕	⬆⬇
❸ Estimates of Variable Consideration	✕	✓	⬆⬇	✕	⬆⬇
❹ Standalone Selling price	✕	✓	⬆⬇	✕	⬆⬇
❺ Timing of Revenue Recognition	✓	✓	⬆⬇	⬆⬇	⬆⬇
❻ Disclosure	✕	✓	✕	⬆	⬇
❼ Licenses	✓	✓	⬆⬇	✕	⬆⬇
❽ Capitalization of Costs	✓	✓	✕	⬇	⬆
❾ Contract Modifications	✕	✓	⬆⬇	⬆⬇	⬆⬇

✕ No impact　✓ Impact　⬆⬇ Positive or negative impact　⬆ Positive impact　⬇ Negative impact

Figure 27　The change for telecommunication companies at a glance

The defense sector is a completely different case than telecommunications. Companies in this sector have a small number of large-volume contracts, instead of a large number of small contracts. In this case, it may be best to implement IFRS 15 with existing functionalities, without a dedicated accounting solution like SAP RAR.

Here are possible ways IFRS 15 can impact companies in the defense sector:

- Contracts are usually long-term, i.e. performed over several accounting periods, even decades,
- Contracts include many elements, such as product development, series production and various services, including warranty, etc,
- The sale of military aircraft with technical support services in one contract will imply multiple Performance Obligations,
- The aspects of contracts that have discounts, rebates, refunds, incentives and penalties will need to be evaluated,
- Revenues will need to be recognized over time with the Percentage of Completion method (PoC),
- Contract modifications might lead to new contracts according to IFRS 15.

Key points, regardless of your industry:

- Each organization should perform a preliminary assessment of how they will be affected by IFRS 15 to determine how to prepare and implement it,
- Entities should consider whether they will need to make changes to accounting policies, accounting systems and internal controls over financial reporting due to regulations in specific jurisdictions.

2.2.3 Business operations

IFRS 15 enables higher transparency and control for organizations, both locally and globally. Therefore, more standardized and centralized business operations must be defined.

Continuing with the example of a telecommunications company, we see that adapting business and operations to IFRS 15 is not only a challenge for the accounting department.

Telecommunications companies, which commonly **subsidize handsets as part of their business models**, will have to reallocate revenue from the service element of the contract to the handset element, based on a relative fair-value calculation. This means higher complexity in revenue accounting, and companies may respond with **new pricing strategies**.

Alternatively, **old business models can be replaced** by new ones that feature financed handsets, where the customer pays for the handset over a period of time and pays to a different legal entity. In this case, the service package is sold to the customer with a separate contract from another legal entity.

In either case, business operations are impacted by IFRS 15 and should be reviewed.

Key point about Business Operations:

- Accounting standards should not dictate to companies how they should run their businesses. Therefore, it's useful to develop a variety of alternatives.

2.2.4 Tax accounting and methods

The impact of IFRS 15 will be country-specific and depends on the tax law in each country.

Keep in mind that:

- Because of changes in the timing of revenue recognition, IFRS impacts how deferred taxes are determined,
- Companies may need to revise transfer pricing strategies and documentation,
- Companies may need updated policies, systems, processes, and controls regarding income tax accounting and financial accounting,
- Sales and/or excise taxes may change because revenue may be re-allocated as product or service revenue.

Key points about tax accounting and methods:

- A company should assess potential changes to financial reporting and tax accounting, if local law is not updated to reflect the requirements of IFRS 15,
- Understand that recognized deferred taxes may be impacted,

2.2.5 Investor relations and communications

Users of financial statements, such as boards of directors, audit committees, analysts, investors, creditors and shareholders need an explanation about changes in the financial statements due to IFRS 15.

For starters, IFRS 15 requires **an increased level of disclosures** about revenue recognition in comparison to previous standards. Disclosures are intended to help users of financial statements with information about the nature, amount, timing and uncertainty of revenue, as well as the cash flows presented in them.

A company's ability to pay dividends to shareholders is impacted by recognized profits, which are affected by the timing of revenue recognition. Depending on local GAAP changes regarding revenue recognition, companies may need to determine if the timing of revenue and profit recognition will change significantly. If so, companies should communicate this to the appropriate stakeholders.

Companies should provide qualitative and quantitative disclosures about their contracts with customers by making clear to stakeholders:

- Any significant judgments made in applying IFRS 15 to contracts,
- Any asset recognized in relation to the cost of obtaining or fulfilling a contract,
- Any updates or changes to the systems or processes required to ensure they are able to comply with the disclosure requirements,
- Impact of first application of IFRS 15 to the financial statements, which transition method and which practical expedients have been used.

2.2.6 Remuneration plans

IFRS 15 is about revenue. Changes in revenue recognition as a result of IFRS 15 may occasionally have an impact on employee bonuses that are linked to revenue or profit.

Compensation and bonus plans which are based on reported revenue or profit may be impacted because of changes to revenue allocation between performance obligations and changes in the timing of revenue recognition.

Sales incentive plans must be reviewed and modified as a result of IFRS 15 as well.

Here are a few key points regarding remuneration plans. The following questions should be analyzed:

- Will adaptations to existing compensation plans be enough, or should a totally new framework be implemented?
- Will the new standard strongly impact the timing of sales targets and the likelihood of those targets being met?
- How will your company ensure consistency and fairness for sales people if a reversal of revenue occurs?

2.2.7 Management information

It's vital for management to be aware and fully understand the impact of IFRS 15 on Key Performance Indicators (KPIs) and financial statements. Existing KPIs should be reviewed and modified in light of IFRS 15:

- As an example, the **average revenue per user (ARPU)** is a common KPI in the telecommunications industry. With the introduction of IFRS 15, some service revenues may be re-allocated to handset sales, which would make ARPU appear lower.
- Companies should make a communications plan that maps out how to introduce changes to the existing KPIs and how to introduce new KPIs to company stakeholders.

For a successful implementation, **operations managers at all levels** should be involved in the rollout and in training, so that the new guidance and modified performance indicators are introduced properly and in a timely fashion.

Your organization needs to consider:

- How will our KPIs be impacted by IFRS 15 adoption?
- Due to the implementation, can and should we make improvements to our management tools and reports, to better monitor company performance?
- How can we ensure stakeholders properly understand the impact of IFRS 15 on our revenues and KPIs?

2.2.8 IT systems

To gather all information required for reporting under IFRS 15, companies may require significant re-designs or modifications to their IT systems, processes, and internal control environment.

Accounting software that delivers information for revenue recognition from billing systems should be customizable to capture new information that was not needed before the new standard was introduced. Your IT solution may need to be modified, remapped, reconfigured or even replaced by a totally new solution to be able to report under IFRS 15. The new accounting system will need to be sufficiently flexible to cope with future changes in pricing and in the variety of product offerings.

The number of IT systems involved makes a difference in the complexity of the transition since key data will have to be gathered from billing, CRM, commissions and data warehouse systems. All this data will have to be collected and connected to enable IFRS 15 contracts to be created and modified.

The new accounting standard **effective date is January 1, 2018**. For those companies that have not yet started with the development and implementation of the modifications needed, time is running short.

Key matters to think about regarding IT systems:

- Are we already collecting all necessary information needed to satisfy IFRS 15 reporting requirements, and is it going to the right places?

- Is our accounting software able to provide answers to the following questions:
  o What is the transaction price and what are the performance obligations?
  o How should revenue be allocated to different goods and services?
  o What is the impact of a contract modification and how should it be calculated?
  o Should contract costs be capitalized, and if yes, how?
  o Should revenue be adjusted for the effects of the time value of money?

2.2.9 Processes

Companies will need to update their financial processes to identify different performance obligations in each contract and pinpoint when and how those obligations are fulfilled under the new revenue recognition guidelines.

With **IFRS 15,** companies will need to consider whether additional performance obligations exist in the contract. This assessment will need to be extended to all obligations under a contract, even items that are not regularly sold by the entity, or items that had previously been seen as unsold items. This means companies may need to modify their whole contract management process.

Also, companies must investigate if certain services/fees meet the definition of **a separate performance obligation** (such as fees for service activation, connection, or installation)**,** and if a good or service has been transferred to the customer. In most cases, companies need to implement whole new IT systems to manage the new performance obligations.

Another aspect to consider is **the timing of revenue recognition**. It will be significantly affected if components of bundled offerings are considered separate performance obligations under IFRS 15. The recognition period could extend beyond the initial contractual term if the customer has the option to renew it. That option provides the customer with a material right.

Key matters to consider regarding processes:

- Are our existing revenue recognition solutions and processes, contract management tools and personnel able to handle the new guidelines? Are improvements to the existing processes sufficient, or should a completely new process framework be designed and implemented?
- How will companies ensure consistency of judgements in identifying all existing performance obligations, estimating stand-alone selling prices, and progress towards completion?
- Will your company need new processes and controls to identify and capitalize incremental contract costs, periodically review contract costs, and test capitalized amounts for impairment? Will it need new processes and controls to estimate variable considerations and determine whether a significant reversal of revenue will occur or not?

2.2.10 Change management

New revenue-recognition guidelines, processes, IT systems and compensation models will have a big impact on your organization and your talent.

Since **implementation of IFRS 15 is time-sensitive**, companies should implement a change-management plan that anticipates the impact of the new standard with policies and systems that will facilitate implementation. In addition, all appropriate leaders should be identified to oversee the adoption.

Training and support: Companies should provide training to all impacted professionals, including accountants, controllers, internal auditors, sales representatives who draw up customer contracts, and the management that uses financial statement information for decision making.

Active discussions with HR: HR should release guidance memos about new compensation policies to all impacted employees.

Key matters to consider regarding change management:

- Those leaders in charge of the implementation project should enable effective coordination among all key functions of the company, for instance tax and accounting, HR, in-house legal (contracting), sales, investor relations, IT and internal audit.

- A company's audit committee and others involved in governance should be included as active participants in the project.

2.3 Challenges on the way to implementing IFRS 15

The authors of this book have supported IFRS 15 implementations in many different companies across various industries, identifying several challenges and potential risks of the transition to IFRS 15. This chapter outlines those risks, challenges and opportunities and presents ideas for addressing each before you even begin with the implementation of IFRS 15.

2.3.1 Data availability and quality

Incomplete data or data with insufficient quality can create a significant risk in your implementation of IFRS 15. If detected during the implementation, this can lead to a delay and re-planning of the project. Especially in large companies with many subsidiaries, the project team must ensure quality and completeness of the data at an early stage of the project. Ideally, an assessment should be conducted before the start of the project.

Companies should acknowledge this risk and take the chance to improve existing processes, data quality, and data availability. This can also be an opportunity to explore how to improve the effectiveness of business intelligence and analytics.

We recommend:

- Using automated data extraction, transition and load capabilities.
- Identifying data gaps early and developing strategies to mitigate the problems that may result from those gaps.

2.3.2 Disclosure changes

Based on your company's selected transition approach (e.g. full retrospective vs. modified retrospective) discussed in Chapter 1.4, you may need to change disclosure reports and processes. This means you may need to maintain dual reporting for a time. The full retrospective approach, for instance, may lead to substantial additional effort to restate accounts in the comparative periods.

The advantages and disadvantages of both approaches are outlined in Chapter 1.4. To enable pro-forma elaboration of previous FYs, and to get a rough estimate of the effort involved in both approaches, we recommend implementing a separate "disclosure changes" work stream.

2.3.3 Multiple work streams and complex PMO efforts

IFRS 15 will affect a variety of stakeholders including people in accounting, IT, tax, compliance, internal audit, and investor relations. We recommend involving top management and representatives from all key departments. Companies should also share an integrated project plan and use centralized and strong project governance through a Project Management Office (PMO).

2.3.4 Aggressive timelines for adoption

The time between the announcement by IFRS of the new standard and its effective date is deceptively long. It gives companies a false sense of security that they will be able to comply on time. We recommend you start as soon as possible with an initial assessment of the impact of IFRS 15 as well as with setting up a project structure.

2.3.5 High volume use cases

Companies should define repeatable processes and use-case profiles. This is especially relevant for telecommunications companies, as they usually have high volumes of customer contracts. Defining repeatable processes and use-case profiles for each standard use case will not only improve the efficiency of the IFRS 15 implementation. This assessment can also be used as an opportunity to analyze existing contracts and to restructure and refine contract structures and agreements.

An overview of SAP Revenue Accounting and Reporting

3

SAP Revenue Accounting and Reporting (SAP RAR) is a comprehensive IT solution to manage complex revenue accounting processes on top of an existing ERP system. The solution is built to automate and simplify the revenue accounting process and is considered a sub ledger within the financial part of the ERP.

It shall ensure that all relevant transactions are captured in the revenue recognition processes in accordance to regulatory requirements (e.g. IFRS 15). SAP RAR is able to integrate revenue data flows from different source systems; e.g. SAP components like the Sales and Distribution module in SAP ECC (ERP Central Component), as well as third-party applications with transactional data, can be connected to SAP RAR.

SAP RAR is a tool to meet legal requirements such as IFRS 15 and provides many options to customize components in accordance to client needs.

In addition, SAP RAR comes with ready-to-use migration programs to support migration efforts and also provides extension options to meet customer-specific migration requirements.

The following chapters provide a general overview of the SAP RAR solution and the related components that can manage complex legal and regulatory requirements.

3.1 Functional/technical requirements to run SAP Revenue Accounting and Reporting

The SAP RAR module is a bolt-on solution to an existing ERP system – whether SAP or third party – and is not able to operate without a supply of operational data for the revenue accounting application. In SAP terms, this setup is called a solution with a sender or operational component.

Within SAP, the following sender components can supply data to SAP RAR:

- SAP Sales and Distribution module within SAP ECC,
- SAP Customer Relationship Management – SAP CRM,
- SAP Hybris Billing – SAP Billing and Revenue Innovation Management (BRIM).

In an SAP environment SAP RAR can be installed on a different system instance (SAP client) than its sender component. In such cases, companies must ensure that all connected systems share the same (harmonized) configuration and master data.

In addition, companies can also integrate SAP RAR with non-SAP sender components, which can be any system for orders and billing. In this case, additional effort will be required to setup integration scenarios and to prepare migration.

One key for the integration with external systems is the identification of required data to be sent to SAP RAR. In addition, the respective master data governance and management processes need to be in place to ensure correct revenue allocation and recognition to the appropriate customer.

3.2 Architecture/Landscape

The SAP RAR module works as a sub ledger to the general ledger. Within SAP, ledgers are used to represent different accounting principles in parallel. SAP posts data to all ledgers, to a specified selection of ledgers, or to a single ledger, according to the customizing settings. SAP RAR additionally creates adjustment postings to specific adjustment accounts (e.g. Contract Assets, Contract Liabilities, Revenue Adjustments) whereas operational applications (e.g. SAP Sales and Distribution) post directly to common accounts (e.g. Revenue, Cash).

The architecture of revenue accounting was designed to decouple revenue accounting posting processes from transactional postings.

The fact that the postings are decoupled does not mean that these processes are not integrated. On the contrary, both processes are highly integrated to ensure that every revenue relevant piece of information is sent to revenue accounting. But decoupling helps to get transparency on the origin of postings in case of problems.

Figure 28 shows on a high level the architectural landscape:

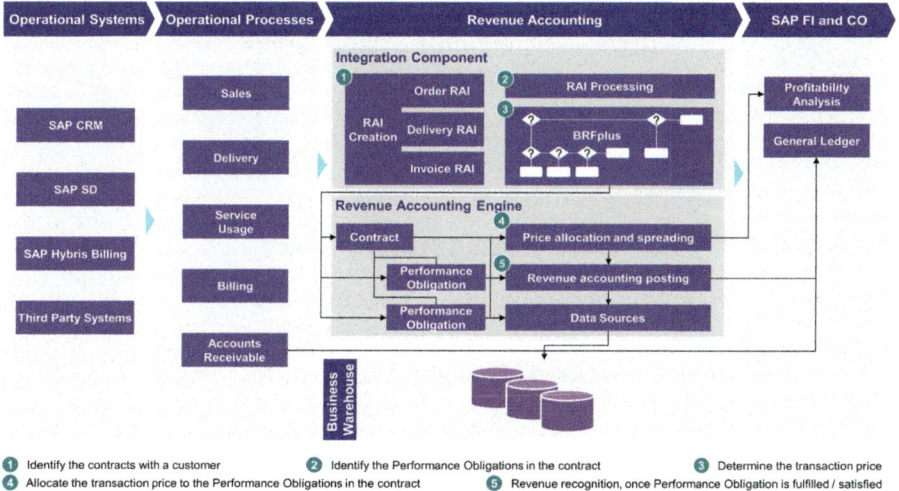

Figure 28   Integration of SAP RAR in the enterprise architecture

3.3 Integration component

As mentioned previously, SAP Revenue Accounting and Reporting requires transactional data as a source to perform revenue accounting processes. In more detail, relevant transactional data must be identified, prepared and processed before revenue accounting processes are executed. These steps take place in the integration component of SAP RAR.

In accordance with the IFRS 15 five-step (see Chapter 1.5) approach, the following steps take place within the integration component:

- IFRS 15 Step 1 – "Identify the contracts with a customer." In accordance to the settings, all transactional data and events that are relevant for revenue accounting are identified and collected for further processing,

- IFRS 15 Step 2 – "Identify the separate performance obligations in the contracts." Collected data is prepared and organized in accordance to the performance obligations (POB) and contracts. Both elements are created once processing of the collected data has been completed,

- IFRS 15 Step 3 – "Determine the transaction price." While collecting and preparing relevant data for revenue accounting, the transaction price is determined.

The upcoming chapters describe how transactional data is identified, prepared and processed within the integration component. In addition, examples of SAP RAR integration with SAP Sales and Distribution and SAP Hybris Billing are provided.

3.3.1 Identify relevant transactional data

Not every transaction occurring in an operational system is relevant for revenue accounting. For example, procurement transactions do not have any impact on revenue recognition and are not relevant for revenue accounting. Typically, every revenue-generating process which is relevant for billing needs to "flow" into revenue accounting. To start with, the implementation team must select which sender components will be used.

After applying the settings, every transaction relevant for revenue accounting will be "detected" by the integration component. The transactional data received will be stored for further processing as a Revenue Accounting Item (RAI).

3.3.2 Revenue Accounting Items – Data preparation for further processing

A RAI is a vehicle for transporting operational data relevant for revenue accounting from a system with transactional data into the revenue accounting engine (Chapter 3.4). This is where revenue accounting processes like allocation and postings take place. As mentioned previously, RAIs are created based on revenue accounting-relevant operational data (e.g. sales order line items). Here RAIs need to be prepared for the revenue accounting requirements. This means that transactional information needs to be organized specifically for the purpose of further processing, and additional information relevant for revenue accounting needs to be derived.

3.3.2.1 Revenue Accounting Item classes

In order to distinguish different transaction types in operational systems, SAP RAR uses so-called Revenue Accounting Item classes. For example, sales orders, deliveries, and invoices result in different RAI classes. This architecture ensures that information received from the operational system is properly prepared for processing in the revenue accounting engine, as each type of transactions requires specific handling. For instance, delivery triggers fulfillment, and invoice transactions create invoicing information relevant for revenue accounting. In other words, the system uses RAI classes to help structure information from the sender components and process it based on class-specific requirements.

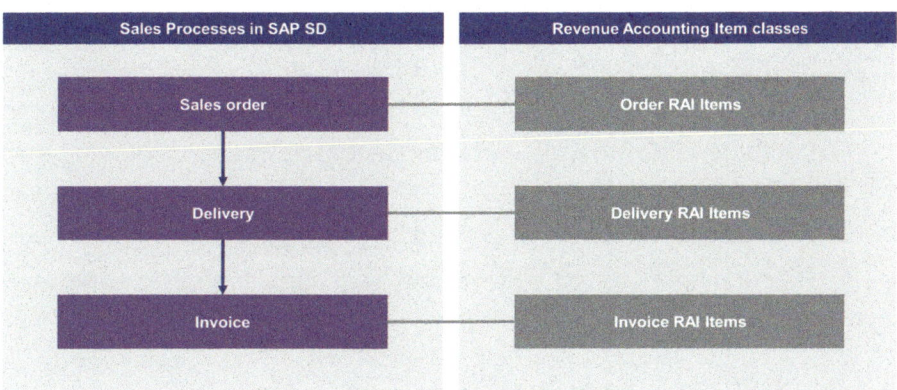

Figure 29   SAP Sales and Distribution Processes mapped to Revenue Accounting Item classes

From a technical perspective, a Revenue Accounting Item class also contains metadata that is required to generate a set of tables and function modules. For each RAI class, there is a separate set of tables and function modules, and the table structures are different for each class.

There are different Revenue Accounting Item classes that correspond to Order RAIs, Delivery RAIs and Invoice RAIs. The three RAI classes are directly correlated to the respective documents in the transactional application. Figure 29 shows the integration with SAP SD. But more importantly, the RAI class also determines the sequence for RAI processing which needs to follow the corresponding sequence in the sender components. This ensures for instance that Invoice RAIs cannot be processed until Delivery and Order RAIs are processed.

In each case, when SAP Revenue Accounting and Reporting is integrated with a SAP sender component, like SAP Sales and Distribution or SAP Hybris Billing, standard Revenue Accounting Item classes similar as described above are used.

However, if SAP Revenue Accounting and Reporting is integrated with another sender application (e.g. a non-SAP sales management application), companies and organizations must define their own Revenue Accounting Item classes to specify technical characteristics that match the specific requirements of sender applications and SAP RAR. When doing so, companies must ensure that the following technical requirements are met after the processing sequence for executing RAI classes has been defined:

- Database tables to store data for custom Revenue Accounting Item classes are created,
- The basic mandatory SAP-defined fields are populated,
- Function modules to receive and save data for custom Revenue Accounting Items are adapted.

3.3.2.2 Revenue Accounting Item status

A processing status is assigned to every Revenue Accounting Item, which indicates how far it has been processed. There are three possible statuses:

- Raw,
- Processable,
- Processed.

RAIs with different statuses are stored in different tables for each class. Whenever a RAI changes status, related data is transferred to the appropriate table. The status can only be changed from "Raw" to "Processable" and from "Processable" to "Processed" and never in the other direction.

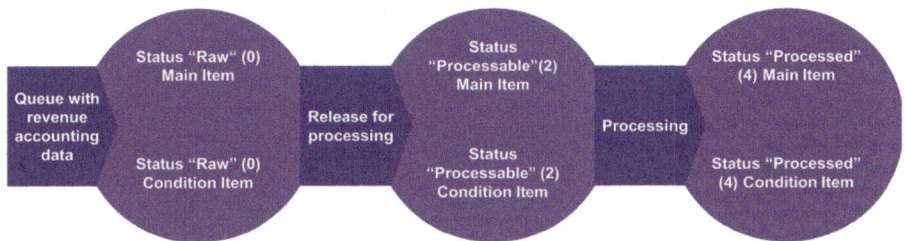

Figure 30   Changes of Revenue Accounting Item status in different process steps

3.3.2.2.1 Revenue Accounting Item status "raw"

Whenever a revenue accounting relevant transaction occurs, a Revenue Accounting Item is created in the "raw" status. This status indicates that information from operational systems has been received but is not yet ready for further processing in the revenue accounting engine. At this stage, received data is already organized by class and includes all relevant raw information from the sender components for further processing. Before RAIs that are "raw" are saved, their content can be modified using specific function modules. For example, the content of the RAI fields can be modified to prepare RAIs from multiple orders for combination into one revenue accounting contract (Multiple Element Arrangement).

All RAIs in the "raw" status must be transferred to the next status – "processable". This requires an additional step, of course. SAP RAR users can decide whether RAIs should be immediately transferred to the "processable" status after creation, or if they should stay in the "raw" status. The choice is a matter of convenience. If automatic transfer of RAIs is enabled, then all RAIs will automatically be saved in the status "processable". Inconsistent data will remain in the "raw" status and must be adjusted before transfer to "processable".

In order to achieve better automation of revenue accounting processes, we recommend activating customizing settings, which ensures that RAIs are directly deemed "processable".

3.3.2.2.2 Revenue Accounting Item status "processable"

As the name of this status indicates, "processable" RAIs are ready to be transferred into the revenue accounting engine. At this stage, all required data from operational systems which has been derived or modified based on custom logic is available. Data for "processable" RAIs has been removed from the "raw" status tables and is now only available in tables for "process-able" RAIs. In the next step, the actual processing of the RAI can be started (Chapter 3.3.2.2.3). If the data is processed successfully, RAI data will be moved from the "processable" status table to the "processed" status table. If an error occurs during RAI processing, then data will not be transferred to the next status and needs to be corrected before processing.

3.3.2.2.3 Revenue Accounting Item status "processed"

After successful processing, information about the processed RAIs is stored in the status "processed", and performance obligations and contracts are created or updated. As per design, data in the status "processed" always includes the latest processed information; it does not include any historical data. For example, if a sales order is created with quantity 1 and a transaction price 126.50 euros, and it is successfully processed but is later changed in the sender component to a quantity of 2 and a transaction price of 253.00 euros, then the new information will be processed and replace the previous entries stored as "processed".

3.3.2.3 Revenue Accounting Item interface

The RAI interface classifies which information is included in an RAI. There are two RAI interfaces: "main" or "condition":

- Main RAIs contain so-called "logistical" information about a Revenue Accounting Item, e.g. the type, start and end dates,
- Condition RAIs show pricing-relevant information, such as the price itself, surcharges, discounts, and further accounting information like the general ledger account.

Both interfaces – "main" and "condition" – are again stored in separate tables for class and status (see Chapter 3.3.2.4).

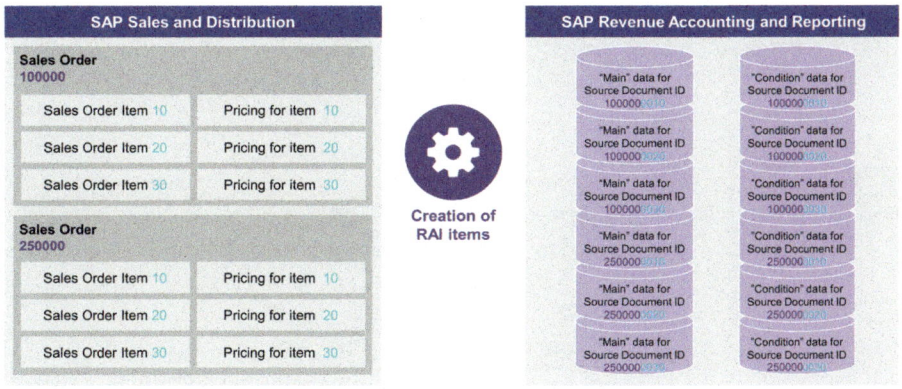

Figure 31   Mapping of sales order item logistical and pricing data to RAI interface type

3.3.2.3.1 Revenue Accounting Item interface "main"

The most important information in the main RAI is the Header ID and the Item ID. These fields are used to map transactional data, e.g. orders and invoices, to Revenue Accounting Items. By using these fields, every RAI can be uniquely assigned to a transactional document and its sales order item. Together, these two fields are used to define a Source Document ID as shown in the diagram below.

Figure 32   Definition of a RAI source document ID

Two other important fields for "main" RAIs are Reference ID and Reference Type. These fields can be modified during RAI creation and are used as explained in this Chapter during RAI processing, to merge RAIs that include multiple orders into one revenue accounting contract (Multiple Element Arrangement).

Figure 33 shows how RAIs of two different orders are handled if the Reference ID and Reference Type fields are not modified. By default, the system sets the Reference ID equal to the sales order number. In this way, it creates one Revenue Accounting contract for each sales order:

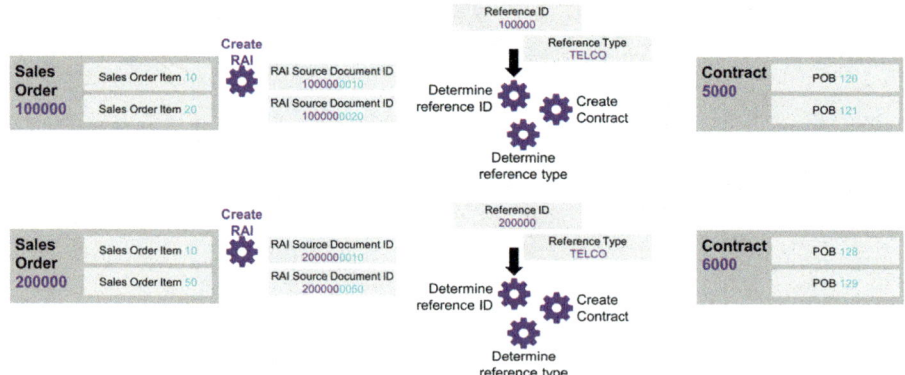

Figure 33   Reference ID and reference type – Impact on revenue accounting contract creation. No contract combination

Figure 34 shows that in case the Reference ID and Reference Type is set to be the same for two sales orders, then one revenue accounting contract for two sales orders will be created:

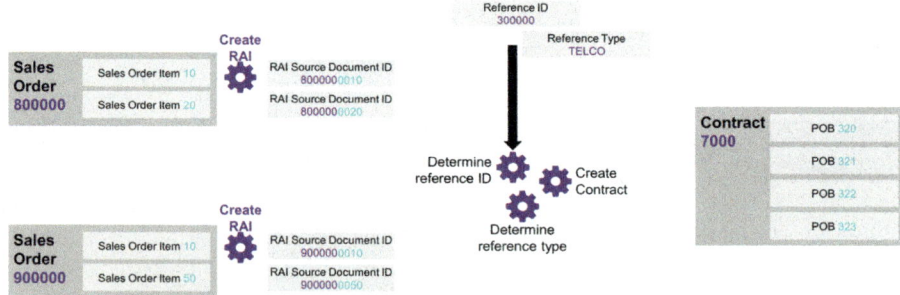

Figure 34   Reference ID and reference type – Impact on revenue accounting contract creation. Contract combination

If multiple orders are not combined into one revenue accounting contract during RAI processing, the user can manually merge multiple contracts after revenue accounting items are processed. Details about contract combination can be found in Chapter 3.4.6.

3.3.2.3.2 Revenue Accounting Item interface "condition"

Condition RAIs contain pricing and accounting information from operational documents. The most important components of a condition RAI are:

- **Source Document ID:** This field is a link between the "main" and "condition" data of an RAI as well as a unique link to one transactional document,
- **Condition Type:** This field includes all revenue accounting relevant conditions. By default, all pricing, discount and surcharge conditions are included. However, during the creation of an RAI, a function module can be used to control which conditions are excluded and included from operational documents. Please note that tax conditions are not relevant for revenue accounting.

At least one "Condition" RAI interface must be flagged as a main condition. Main conditions are usually top-level conditions from the pricing scheme of a transactional document. The main condition includes a value before discounts and surcharges are applied. In case no main condition has been set, the system will generate an error message during RAI processing.

3.3.2.4 Naming convention of RAI tables

Now that we have introduced the concepts of class, status and interface for RAIs, we want to give an overview of the involved database tables and the data flow. The following naming convention for standard RAI tables applies, if SAP RAR is integrated with the SAP Sales and Distribution module:

/1RA/0{RAI_Class}{RAI_Status}{Interface}

RAI Class:

SD01 – Order class,

SD02 – Delivery class,

SD03 – Invoice class.

RAI Status:

0 – Raw status,

2 – Processable status,

4 – Processed status.

RAI Interface:

MI – Main item,

CO – Condition item.

An example of an RAI table which includes unprocessed, main order RAI items is /1RA/0SD012MI.

Figure 35 shows how RAI tables are used in an integrated SAP SD process, which includes sales orders and invoices. The RAIs are created immediately in the status "Processable".

"Processable" RAI data is not transferred to the "processed" status if errors occur during RAI processing.

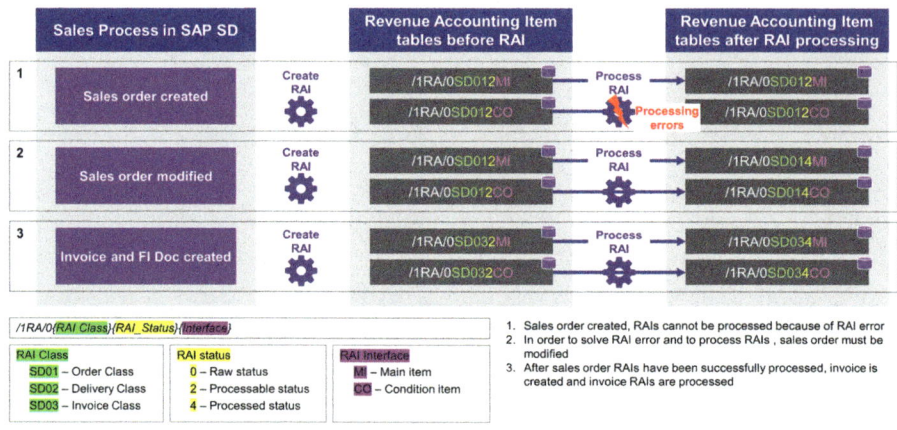

Figure 35   Use of RAI tables with an integrated sales process based on SAP SD

3.3.3 RAI processing

After Revenue Accounting Items have been created, transactional data relevant for revenue accounting is now ready for further processing. In the next step, revenue accounting contracts and performance obligations are created, since RAIs do not include all information relevant for revenue accounting (e.g. special revenue accounting G/L accounts). For this reason, RAIs are enriched with additional information during processing. This is typically done using Business Rule Framework Plus functionality, which allows users to define business rules to derive and determine all required information for performance obligations and contracts (see Figure 36).

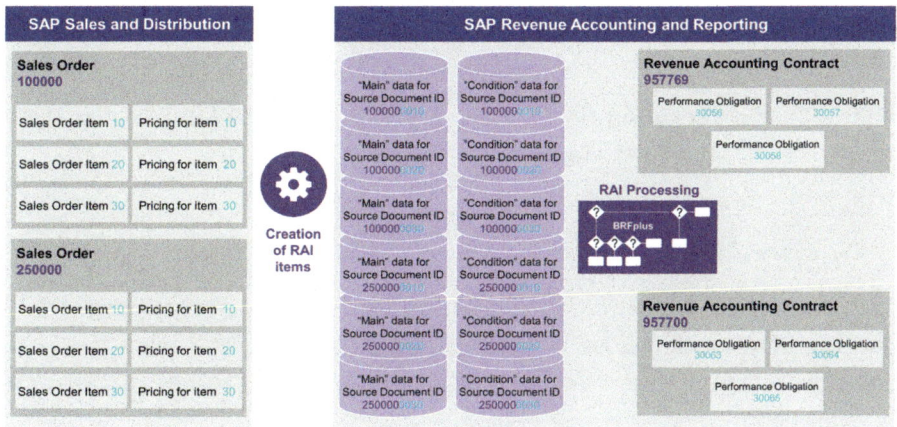

Figure 36   Overview of RAI processing for SAP SD sales orders

This chapter continues with an overview of Business Rule Framework Plus (BRFplus) used during RAI processing, as well as details on the execution of RAI processing.

3.3.3.1 Business Rule Framework Plus

Business Rule Framework Plus (BRFplus) is a SAP tool for defining and processing business rules. It provides a comprehensive application-programming interface and user interface which enables the definition of business rules in an intuitive way. Furthermore, it enables close collaboration between IT and the business during definition of the business rules for an application.

BRFplus is used in SAP Revenue Accounting and Reporting to define processing rules for incoming transactional data, e.g. data received from the SAP Sales and Distribution module. When data is processed into revenue accounting contracts and performance obligations, BRFplus enriches the incoming data with additional information which was not available in the sender application, or it follows specific processing rules to create revenue accounting contracts and performance obligations as required.

3.3.3.1.1 BRFplus overview

Business Rule Framework Plus (BRFplus) enables business users and developers to interact with the rule engine via a graphical web user interface ("workbench"). Within the workbench, implementation and adoption of the rules takes place.

Technical objects within BRFplus can have multiple dimensions; the most important for understanding BRFplus are:

- Data objects, and
- Expressions.

Data objects are similar to the DDIC (Data Dictionary) elements of the ABAP development stack (tables, structures and elements). Their main task is to describe data and to serve as a vehicle for transporting results of an action or expression.

Expressions are responsible for calculation and determination of a result. They are used for storing defined logic within BRFplus, and they provide flexibility.

Expressions have many ways to use existing developments out of the ABAP/ HANA development stack or to support a rule configuration. To make complex expressions transparent for business users and developers, Decision Table Expressions are used. An import and export functionality into a native Microsoft Excel file is supported as a standard functionality of BRFplus. This important feature makes it easy to maintain business rules within the Decision Tables and keep them transparent.

Expressions and data objects are used to define the rule which represents business logic to be applied in a particular business case. Rules "know" the conditions defined by Expressions and can differentiate between two actions – true and false. The complexity of the rules is determined by its Expressions.

Rules are not used as stand-alone objects. Instead, rules must be combined into a ruleset, which represents a collection of all rules (and therefore

Expressions) to be executed in a particular business case. Rulesets represent the top level of the elements which contain computational logic.

To use the BRFplus features out of the application code (ABAP stack), functions are required. A function acts like an interface between the application and the ruleset where the logic is located. It passes the data (context) from the application to the ruleset where the data is processed. Finally, after processing, it returns the results back to the application. BRFplus functions may have only one resulting data object which can be a complex data object that may have impact on the decision-making process.

How the different layers between ABAP OO (Object Oriented) and BRFplus compare are shown in Figure 37:

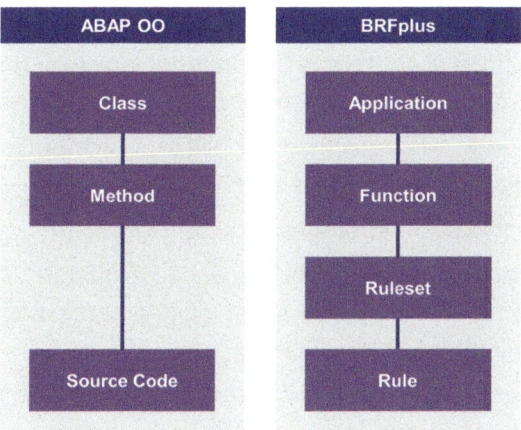

Figure 37   Comparison of layers between ABAP OO and BRFplus

One main difference between ABAP OO and BRFplus is that changes to BRFplus are made within the rules and rulesets. Since the business logic and the technical coding logic are separated, programming skills are not needed to change the logic.

Technically, all implemented rules are contained in customizing tables. During the first execution of the BRFplus rules, ABAP OO code is generated automatically based on the customizing performed and subsequently executed.

All BRFplus applications can be used as local applications or are assigned to a software component which requires handling via transports. Users are offered flexibility on how to handle changes for their BRFplus applications.

3.3.3.1.2 BRFplus in SAP Revenue Accounting and Reporting

Within SAP Revenue Accounting and Reporting, BRFplus is part of the integration component. As described above, within this component, processing of the Revenue Accounting Items (received from sender components, e.g. the SAP Sales and Distribution module) into revenue accounting contracts and performance obligations takes place.

In this step, BRFplus plays a central role. It is used to define rules for the transformation of Revenue Accounting Items into performance obligations and contracts.

Rules defined in BRFplus are used for:

- Determination if an item is "distinct" or not (e.g. it is distinct if the customer can benefit from the good or service on its own),
- Determination of performance obligation attributes, such as review reason, deferral method and even POB name,
- Determination of contract header attributes,
- Determination of linked performance obligations. Linked POBs are sublevel POBs created as a result of RAI processing. Such POBs are always "linked" to leading POBs,
- Determination of a stand-alone selling price, in case it is not supplied as a pricing condition from a sender component,
- Determination of G/L accounts for revenue accounting processing.

In fact, the BRFplus application contains all relevant settings for processing Revenue Accounting Items into performance obligations. Within the BRFplus application, users can define their own processing rules to tailor POB creation to the needs of their organization.

SAP RAR includes ready-to-use BRFplus application templates for integration with the SAP Sales and Distribution module, SAP Hybris Billing, SAP CRM, and any other sender component. Each of these templates includes functions relevant for RAI processing specified by the sender components (this is done through the assignment of the BRFplus application to RAI classes).

Rules and functions within the standard BRFplus applications that are delivered with SAP RAR cannot be changed because it is common practice within SAP products to not allow it. Values/conditions in decision tables can be adjusted.

If changes in the BRFplus application are required, users have to rely on standard BRFplus rules. By doing this, new RAI processing rules, structure fields and decision tables are created based on a robust template.

3.3.3.2 Execution of RAI processing

Revenue Accounting Items can be processed in periodically scheduled jobs or manually through an RAI monitor transaction.

The RAI monitor is a tool that allows the user to display and analyze Revenue Accounting Items and process them into the RAR module to generate or change contracts and performance obligations. The RAI monitor displays revenue accounting items based on specific selection criteria. For example, a user can select RAI items to be processed by class type, the status of an RAI, the company code or the sales order ID.

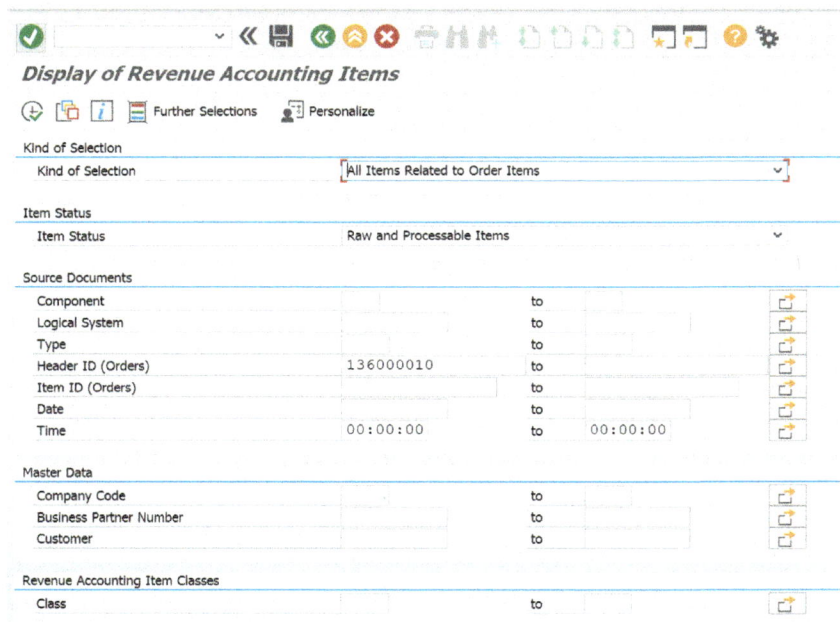

Figure 38   SAP RAR: Selection screen of revenue accounting RAI monitor

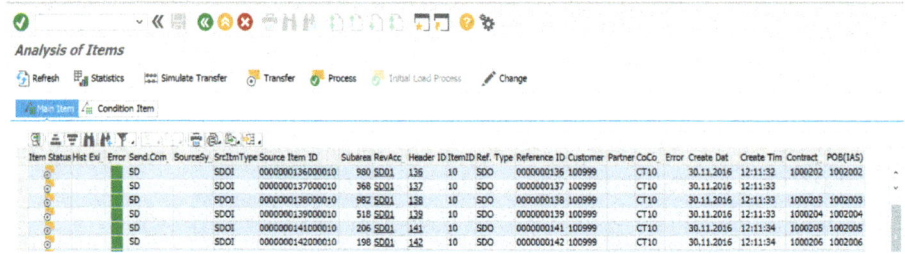

Figure 39   SAP RAR: RAI monitor – Main items

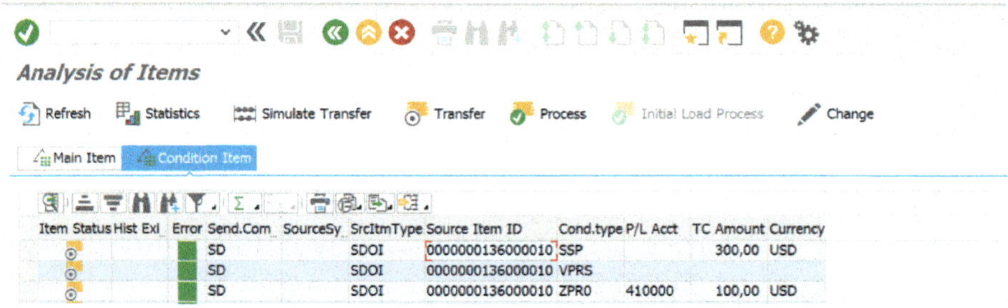

Figure 40   SAP RAR: RAI monitor – Condition items

If used, the Revenue Accounting Item monitor allows users to perform different actions such as:

- Simulate or process Revenue Accounting Items from the raw status to the "processable" status,

- Change "processable" revenue accounting main and/or condition items. Typically, such changes are performed only if data absolutely needs to be changed one time. Otherwise, changes should be applied in the sender component (e.g. SAP SD),

- Process "processable" Revenue Accounting Items.

In order to achieve the best automation results, we recommend processing RAIs with a periodic job. This will process all RAIs with a specific selection criteria at a set time. RAIs that contain errors would have to be fixed before the next scheduled RAI processing run, otherwise they will not be processed once again.

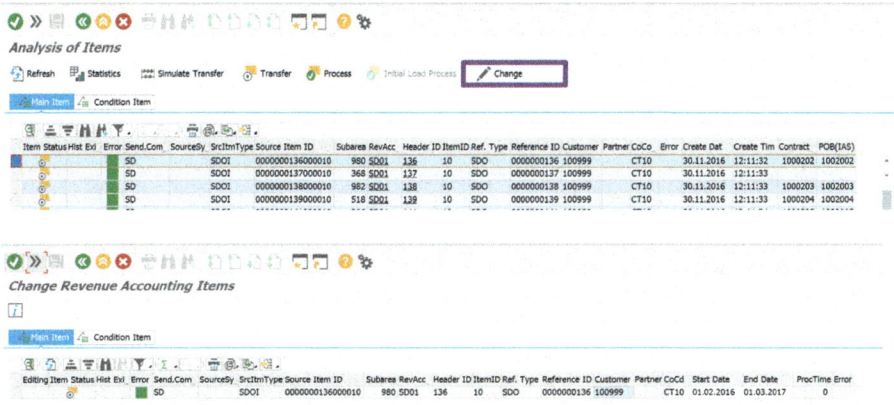

Figure 41   SAP RAR: Change RAIs in RAI monitor

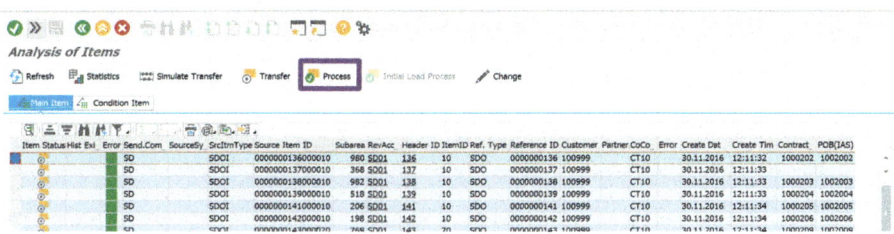

Figure 42   SAP RAR: Process RAI in RAI monitor

If the program is terminated (dump) during RAI processing, no RAIs which have been selected for processing will be processed into revenue accounting. Any object causing the program to terminate (e.g. single RAI objects) would have to be excluded from RAI processing if the root cause of the problem is not resolved.

RAI processing is a very important step in revenue accounting processes since it creates and updates contracts and performance obligations. We recommend doing it on a daily basis and monitoring the results to ensure that transactional data are transferred to revenue accounting for further processing.

3.3.4 Integration with SAP ECC Sales and Distribution

The primary sales-related processes, like the generation of sales orders, delivery notices and invoices within SAP ECC, take place in the Sales and Distribution module. Without using SAP Revenue Accounting and Reporting, revenues would be recognized immediately after invoice creation. In this case, the full amount of an invoice line item without allocation to the other items is recorded to the revenue and receivables account.

In accordance with IFRS 15, revenue allocation needs to take place based on defined rules. To enable rule-based revenue recognition in SAP ECC, the Sales and Distribution module is integrated with the SAP Revenue Accounting and Reporting module. This integration is the technical enablement for revenue reposting in accordance with different revenue recognition standards, such as IFRS 15.

SAP Sales and Distribution integrated with SAP Revenue Accounting and Reporting allows revenue accounting to reverse application postings made with the sales invoice in the general ledger. Revenue recognition instead takes place based on specified rules which are defined for every accounting principle (e.g. IFRS 15). For example, based on rules, revenue starts to be recognized over the contract term.

Below we outline how income generated from a software license sale is handled with SAP RAR:

- Using a customer relationship application, like SAP CRM, a sales agent creates presales data for a customer,
- The sales agent presents an offer to a customer,
- The agent makes a sale and creates a contract with a customer. This contract contains a contractual agreement, such as the contract duration, price, payment terms, and delivery methods. Usually all this information is kept in an object called a sales order. Such a sales order can be created in CRM applications or directly in the SAP Sales and Distribution module. Our example assumes that sales orders are created in SAP CRM and are replicated to SAP Sales and Distribution,
- When a CRM sales order is replicated, the sales data is transferred to the SAP ECC Sales and Distribution module. In that module, it is now possible to issue invoices for each item on the billing plan,

Figure 43   Order replication between SAP CRM and SAP SD

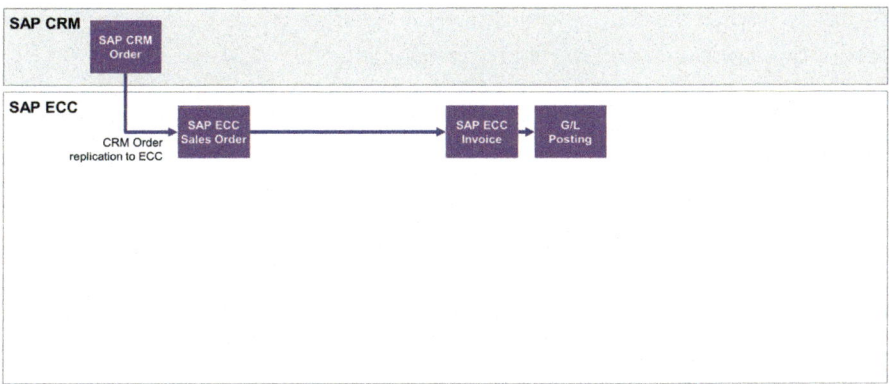

Figure 44   Invoice creation and GL posting

- Once an invoice is created according to the billing plan, postings to the revenue account and receivable account will be created.

In a scenario where SAP Sales and Distribution is integrated with SAP Revenue Accounting and Reporting, order creation, order updates, as well as invoice creation and cancellation, including debit and credit notes, will create Revenue Accounting Items.

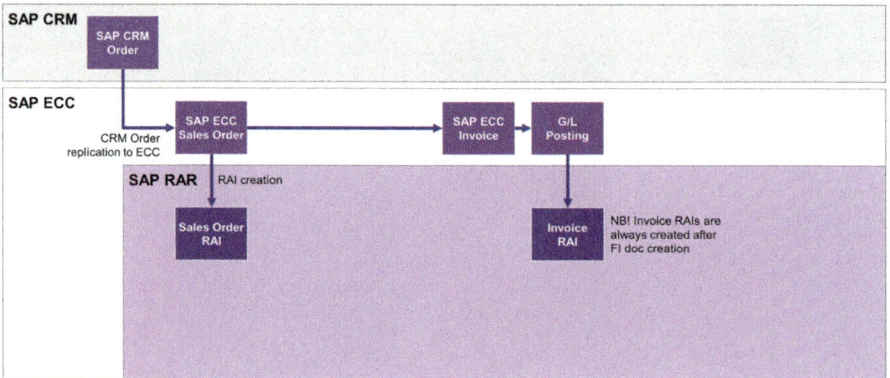

Figure 45   Creation of Revenue Accounting Items

Business analysts are able to review the newly created revenue accounting contracts and performance obligations if needed. More details on revenue accounting contracts and performance obligations follow in Chapter 3.4.1.

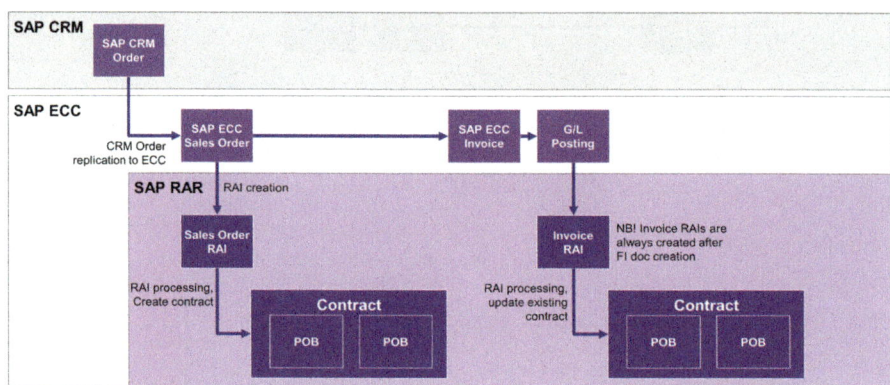

Figure 46   Processing of Revenue Accounting Items and creation of contract and POBs

In the next steps, revenue accounting contracts are reviewed and manually changed (e.g. contracts are combined, or revenues are manually spread over the duration of a POB) if required. If no changes are needed, the contracts are prepared for revenue posting in finance. This posting, as mentioned above, reverses the postings done during invoice creation (in SAP Sales and Distribution). Revenue is then recognized in accordance with the allocation and spreading logic performed within the revenue accounting tool.

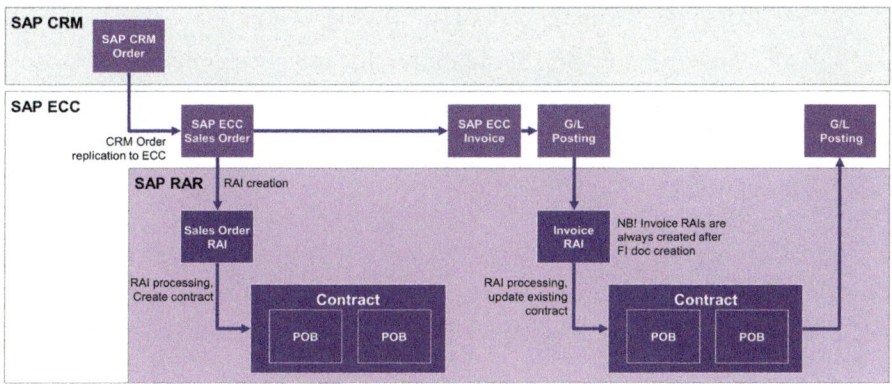

Figure 47   Revenue Accounting posting to General Ledger

In addition, SAP RAR lets users combine different customer contracts into one revenue accounting contract, so that the revenue can be recognized automatically for all products and services sold to a single customer. This flexibility and the allocation rules are not possible in the SAP Sales and Distribution module.

In other words, SAP Revenue Accounting and Reporting integrated with SAP Sales and Distribution helps perform revenue recognition applying automated allocation logic among different elements of multiple customer contracts.

3.3.5 Integration with SAP Hybris Billing (BRIM)

The SAP Hybris Billing solution (formerly known as Billing and Revenue Innovation Management – BRIM) is designed to help customers manage high volumes of billing. This solution is part of SAP Customer Engagement and Commerce (CEC) and is commonly used with subscription and use-based business models. For example, utilities and telecommunications companies often use SAP Hybris Billing.

SAP Hybris Billing consists of the following software components:

- SAP CRM for subscription order management,
- SAP Convergent Mediation by Digital Route for Billing Mediation and Service Control processes,

- SAP Convergent Charging (CC) for pricing/charging,
- SAP Convergent Pricing Simulation – for pricing simulation purposes,
- SAP Flexible Solution Billing,
- Convergent Invoicing (CI) and Contract Accounts Receivable and Payable both in SAP ERP (FI-CA).

A typical scenario for SAP Hybris Billing is using SAP CRM, Convergent Charging (integrated into ERP through web services), Convergent Invoicing (CI) and Contract Accounts Receivable and Payable (FI-CA) in ERP.

In CI, provider contracts and billable items are captured and invoiced. Provider contracts are the source of transactional data for SAP Revenue Accounting and Reporting. The invoice information comes from billable items. This makes Convergent Invoicing the integration centerpiece between SAP Hybris Billing and SAP RAR.

The Convergent Invoicing component "feeds" the revenue accounting module with all relevant information. In other words, when SAP Hybris Billing is integrated, Convergent Invoicing acts as a sender component. It sends data to the integration component, where Revenue Accounting Items (RAI) are created. RAIs are then processed into revenue accounting which creates and updates the revenue accounting contracts.

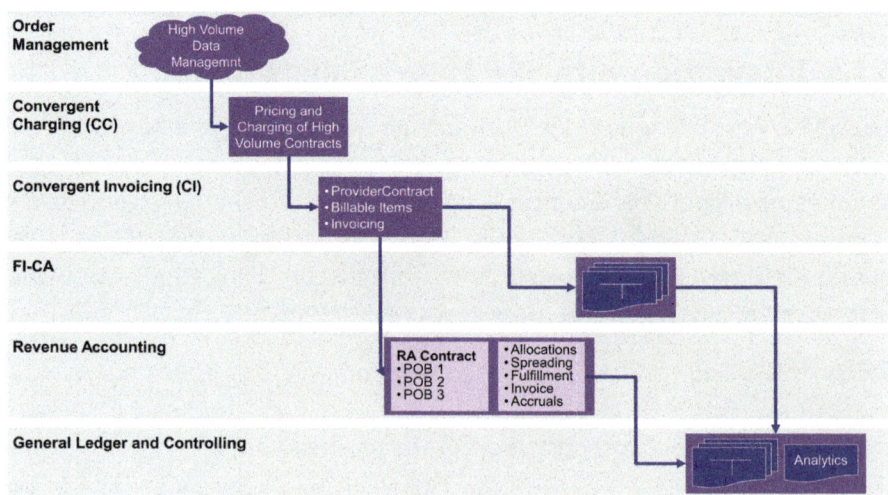

Figure 48   SAP Revenue Accounting and Reporting integration with SAP Hybris Billing

Figure 48 shows an integration scenario between SAP Hybris Billing and SAP Revenue Accounting and Reporting.

3.4 Revenue accounting engine

After relevant contracts with customers have been identified (IFRS 15 Step 1 – "Identify the contracts with a customer") and Revenue Accounting Items have been created, processing of RAIs takes place. At this point, revenue accounting contracts and performance obligations are created (IFRS 15 Step 2 – "Identify the separate performance obligations in the contracts"). Then transaction prices are determined for all contracts created (IFRS 15 Step 3 – "Determine the transaction price").

The main elements needed for revenue accounting are now available, and actual revenue recognition can take place. All the following processes take place in a so-called revenue accounting engine. It is a centerpiece of the revenue accounting application, and the engine performs the following high-level processes:

- Calculation of price allocation and default spreading (IFRS 15 Step 4 "Allocate the transaction price to the performance obligations within the contract"),
- Calculation of invoice correction effects,
- Calculation of recognized revenue based on fulfillment events,
- Creation of posting data and execution of posting run,
- IFRS 15 Step 5 – "Revenue recognition, once performance obligation is fulfilled/satisfied",
- Reporting and data provisioning for the Business Warehouse (BW).

The following will provide details on the revenue accounting engine.

3.4.1 Revenue accounting objects

As discussed, the revenue accounting module handles two main types of objects: contracts and their performance obligations (POBs). RAI processing leads to the creation and update of contracts and performance obligations.

Revenue accounting contracts have one or more performance obligations.

The revenue accounting contract represents a top-level object in revenue accounting. It can consist of one or multiple elements, which include items converted to performance obligations. In case SAP Revenue Accounting and Reporting is integrated with SAP Sales and Distribution, by default, the revenue accounting contract is always created for each sales order relevant for revenue accounting.

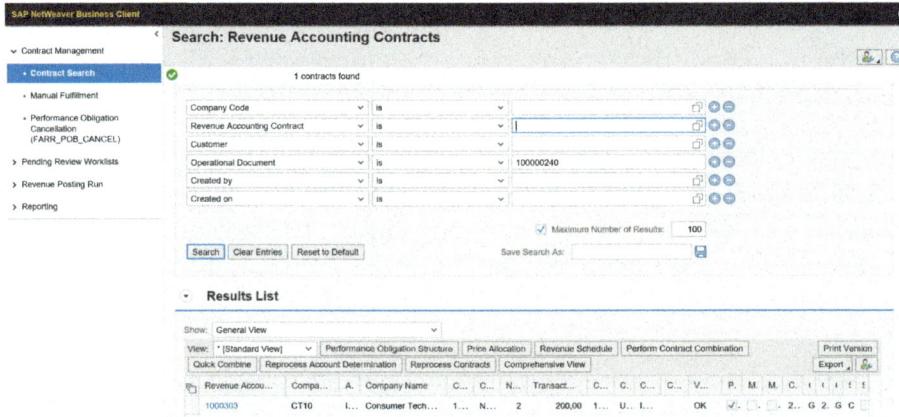

Figure 49   SAP RAR: Contract search. Search contracts by operational documents

Performance obligations can be bundled into a multi-level structure with headers and sub-header items. In the standard view ("List view") of the Revenue Accounting user interface, the user is not able to see the hierarchy of performance obligations – only the underlying performance obligations are visible.

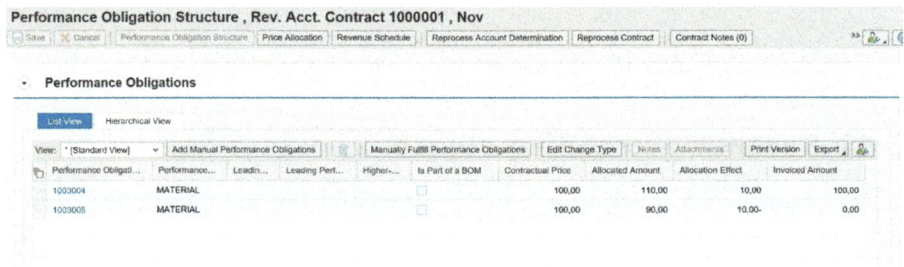

Figure 50   SAP RAR: Performance Obligation Structure List view

In order to see the hierarchy of the contract, the user has to select the "Hierarchical View". In case POBs have been created for products structured as Bills of Material (BOM), a corresponding hierarchy will be displayed.

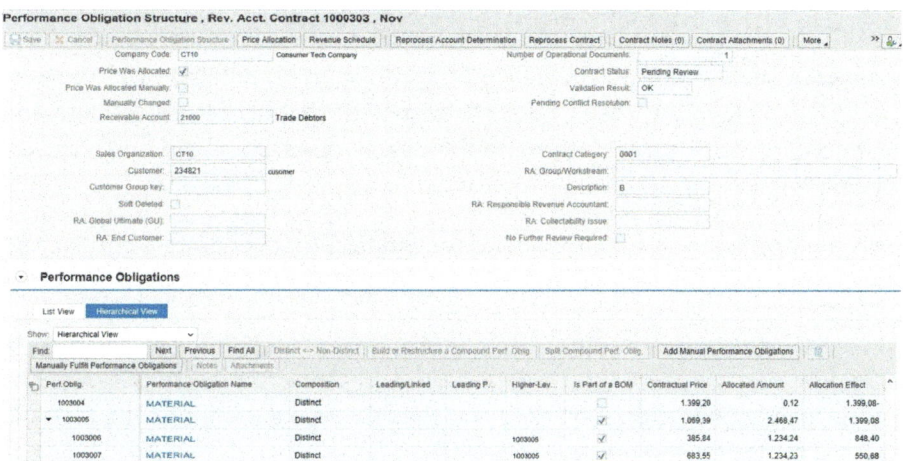

Figure 51   SAP RAR: Performance Obligation structure hierarchical view

In addition to the POBs that are created and updated after RAI processing, users can create manual POBs which do not have any link to the operational data and do not contain transaction prices. Such POBs are created for allocation purposes.

3.4.2 Revenue recognition methods

SAP Revenue Accounting and Reporting is able to handle multiple revenue accounting recognition methods. A revenue recognition method is a particular way of performing the recognition process for a performance obligation.

The three most common recognition methods are:

- **Time-based recognition:** Recognition based on the revenue received every month for the duration of the contract,
- **Percentage of completion:** Recognition of the revenue based on a specified percentage typically related to actual progress vs. plan. This is also known as manual fulfillment,

- **Event-based fulfillment:** Revenue recognition based on an event. For example, revenue recognition may be based on a "goods issue" event or customer invoice.

3.4.2.1 Time-based revenue recognition

A revenue accounting performance obligation can be fulfilled over a certain period of time. In this case, the performance obligation has a start date and an end date. Both dates determine the overall duration of the performance obligation.

This method handles fulfillment and recognition that generate a certain revenue in each accounting period.

Each performance obligation with time-based recognition has a revenue schedule that contains the revenue values of the appropriate periods. The performance obligation start date and the POB end date define the first and the last period of the revenue schedule.

There are different ways to spread the revenues over the periods of the revenue schedule. Either the system calculates the values automatically, or the user manually enters the revenues (Details in section 3.4.4.2) so that manual spreading takes place.

The invoiced amount of a performance obligation with time-based recognition within a given period can be higher or lower than recognized revenue. In case of overstatement (revenue is higher than the invoice), the system generates a "liability" entry in the posting table. In case of understatement (invoice is higher than revenue), the system generates an "asset" entry in the posting table (also see Chapter 1.6).

For example, time-based revenue recognition can be used if the full value of goods or services sold cannot be taken immediately as revenue. This can be the case for instance when maintenance service is sold.

3.4.2.2 Percentage of completion

The Revenue Accounting module is also able to handle the fulfillment of performance obligations based on percentage of completion (PoC).

A good example for percentage of completion use in revenue accounting can be a fixed-price project.

In this case, the overall project price is fixed and the progress of completion is measured through achievement of defined project phases. For example, once the requirements analysis phase is completed, the service provider can recognize 15% of the overall fixed price. In the revenue accounting module, the percentage of completion for a corresponding performance obligation would have to be changed to 15%. This would mean that 15% of the overall fixed price would be scheduled for revenue posting in the current month (assuming that revenue postings for this POB are not suspended).

Further, an invoice for the services provided will be issued. In case the invoicing follows the completion of project phases, then revenue and invoicing amount would be the same.

However, as in the case of time-based revenue recognition, the invoiced amount of a performance obligation with PoC recognition can overstate or understate the current stage of completion. In case of overstatement, the system generates a "liability" entry in the posting table. In the case of understatement, the system generates an "asset" entry in the posting table (see Chapter 1.6).

Percentage of completion is also called manual fulfillment, since users have the option to manually adjust/change the percentage amount to be recognized. It is also possible to enter negative percentage values to reverse fulfillments.

3.4.2.3 Event-based recognition

The fulfillment of a revenue accounting performance obligation can also be triggered by a certain event, such as a goods issue, customer invoice or corresponding reversal transactions. Reversal transactions happen when goods are returned and the invoice is cancelled.

Event-based fulfillment is used when it's clear that revenue can be recognized immediately after an event, for example when a manufactured product is delivered or time and material consulting services are invoiced.

3.4.3 Stand-alone selling price

The stand-alone selling price (SSP) is the price an entity would charge for a service or product if such a product were sold individually.

The stand-alone selling price is used in revenue accounting to determine the allocation amount of every performance obligation included in each contract (see Chapter 1.5.4).

The SSP provided for the revenue accounting engine is the basis for POBs. If required, the SSP can be changed manually for each performance obligation created.

Usually, the SSP is determined by comparing input values, such as the floor price and renewal rate.

The rules for determining the SSP can be defined using pricing settings in the SAP Sales and Distribution module or with the BRFplus:

- For example, users can set a specific pricing condition to determine the SSP in SAP SD. This condition will be sent to revenue accounting during RAI processing. The performance obligation in revenue accounting then uses this condition as the SSP,
- If BRFplus is used, decision rules would have to be defined in the system. If activated, BRFplus becomes the only basis for determining the SSP. For example, a decision table with a material code, the floor price and additional logic can be used to determine the SSP.

3.4.4 Price allocation

In revenue accounting, "allocation" means the distribution of values between two or more performance obligations in a contract. After allocation, the POB is changed to reflect the allocated amount.

The revenue accounting module allows you to allocate transaction prices among performance obligations in a revenue accounting contract. By default, price allocation is based on stand-alone selling prices, but custom price allocation logic can be implemented with BAdI, which stands for Business Add-In.

Price allocation can only happen on distinct POBs that are not excluded from price allocations. This happens within a contract, based on specific logic.

This functionality ensures allocation for all applicable POBs is in accordance with the underlying rule set (e.g. IFRS 15).

3.4.4.1 Price allocation based on stand-alone selling price

Usually, price allocation is based on a stand-alone selling price (SSP). As previously discussed, a SSP is supplied by a sender component (e.g. SAP Sales and Distribution) or is calculated during RAI processing with the help of BRFplus. Once a contract is created, the SSP is used to distribute the overall transaction price of a contract to all performance obligations which were not excluded from price allocation.

This type of price allocation is one of the most convenient, since the standard logic of price allocation can remain unchanged, even if BRFplus is applied.

In addition, users can implement their own allocation logic using Business Add-In's (BAdI's) available in the standard solution. For example, a contract can be split into 70% for one group of performance obligations and 30% for another group within a contract. In this case, the standard allocation logic based on a stand-alone selling price is "overruled".

3.4.4.2 Manual price allocation

In cases which are not covered by an implemented standard and/or custom allocation logic, users must adjust the allocation results individually for a given contract with a manual allocation functionality. Users might need to adjust price allocation manually for several reasons, including an individual contract revenue split or a carve-out of revenue. Manual allocation functionality provides users a framework for changing allocations based on their needs.

Any manual allocation changes within a contract will be saved and according to default settings, the system will "safeguard" the manual changes. For example, if price allocation based on an SSP has been changed manually within a contract and a new set of revenue accounting items is processed, then a revenue accounting engine receives SSPs which are not correct, according

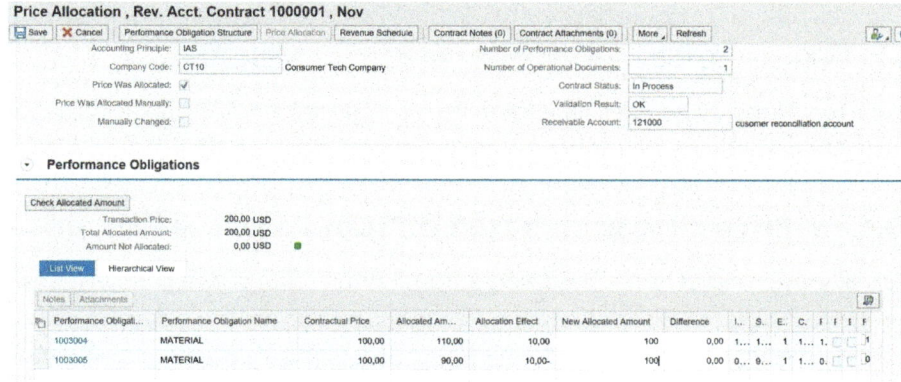

Figure 52   SAP RAR: Manual price allocation

to the current contract allocation. In this case, the manual allocation previously performed by a user is kept, and the contract is deemed "In Conflict" (more about conflict handling in Chapter 3.5). Using the conflict worklist, the user can solve the conflict by selecting to keep manual allocation, or by accepting the changes received from the sender component. In case of price changes, the system will offer an overview about the situation before and after the last change from the sender component so that the user can adjust the values accordingly.

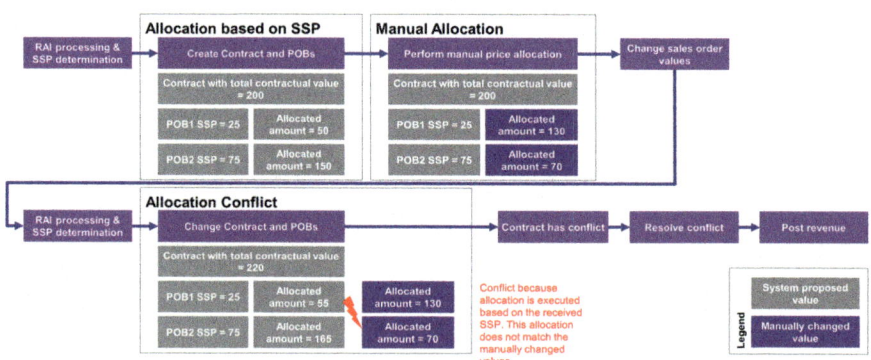

Figure 53   Example of manual price allocation and its effect on the revenue accounting contract processing

As discussed, manual price allocation changes can lead to conflicts which need to be resolved manually. This can be a time-consuming task, depending on the origin and complexity of the conflicts. Hence, it is always better to limit the number of manual changes.

3.4.5 Spreading

Price allocation is the allocation of a contract transaction price among performance obligations within the contract. Spreading describes the distribution of the revenues across the periods (months) within one performance obligation. Spreading is only relevant for time-based performance obligations, because it can only be performed across the periods of a POB. In other words, the revenue schedules for contracts with time-based recognition contain all accounting periods within the contract duration (e.g. the start and end dates of time-based POBs). The fulfillment of the performance obligations is determined by the distribution of revenues over the contract duration – the so-called spreading.

Revenue accounting is able to handle three different ways of determining the spreading of a performance obligation. In the next chapters, we explain these three types.

3.4.5.1 Spreading based on standard distribution logic

One way to determine how the system spreads the fulfillment of a performance obligation over the contract duration is the deferral method. There are different deferral methods available, such as:

a. **Linear Distribution:** The system distributes the fulfillment of the performance obligation over a number of days specified by the contract start and end date of a POB (e.g. contract duration). The recognized revenue for each accounting period is in proportion to the number of days that belong to the accounting period. This leads to evenly distributed revenues.

   Depending on the requirements, revenue accounting can also calculate spreading based on 365/366 or 360 days.

b. **Recognition in first period:** Fulfillment of POB will happen in the first period only.

c. **Recognition in end period:** The system puts all revenue into the last accounting period of the duration in order to fulfill the performance obligation.

3.4.5.2 Spreading based on custom logic

In some situations, customers might need to spread the fulfillment of a performance obligation in a way that cannot be covered with one of the above described deferral methods. In such cases, SAP Revenue Accounting and Reporting offers a Business Add-In (BAdI) to develop custom spreading logic. It is important to note that the custom logic can only be implemented for time-based fulfillment POBs, since other fulfillment types like Event Based or Manual Fulfillment (percentage of completion) have their own logic, which are included in the standard program code.

Custom spreading logic might be required for maximum or minimum limits within a month, or when time-based revenue recognition should be performed based on a decreasing or increasing schedule.

For example, companies must recognize a certain amount per month regardless of the start date of a time-based POB.

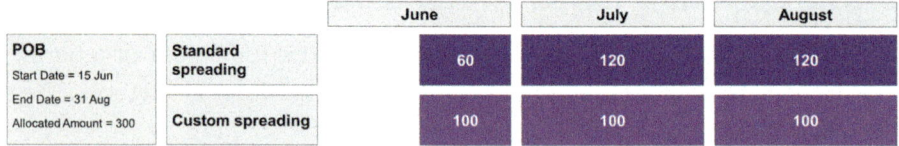

Figure 54 Difference between standard spreading and custom-logic spreading

3.4.5.3 Manual spreading

The manual spreading functionality can be used for performance obligations that need manual adjustment. Here it is possible to distribute the revenue over each accounting period within the duration. In this way, default spreading is overwritten through manual input.

Similar to manual price allocation, manual spreading can result in changed values that do not match the data received from the sender component after the last RAI processing. For example, after manual spreading changes, pricing

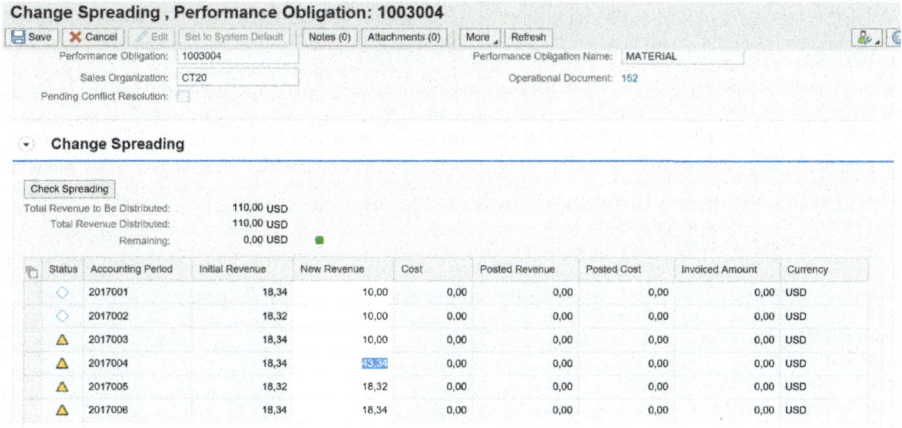

Figure 55   SAP RAR: Change spreading manually

changes in the operational system have occurred. This creates different RAIs to be processed. The revenue accounting engine will then apply the standard and/or custom logic for spreading. However, it will detect that spreading was adjusted manually and will not overwrite the manual changes (according to a default set in this way). This will result in a conflict that will be put on the conflict worklist. The user can finally solve the conflict by keeping the manual spreading or by accepting the changes received from the sender component. In case of price changes, the system will provide an overview of the "before" and "after" status.

Manual spreading and allocation can lead to many conflicts that take a long time to resolve. Therefore, we advise companies to minimize the number of manual changes in revenue accounting applications.

3.4.6 Contract combination

The first step in the 5-step model of revenue recognition in IFRS 15 is the identification of the contracts with the customers.

The goal here is to identify elements which belong together and which share common attributes so they can be combined into one revenue accounting contract for transaction price calculation and allocation purposes.

When elements originate in different objects (e.g. sales orders) from one or different operational applications, the elements can be combined into one revenue accounting contract. For example, when sales orders for services and products are created separately, multiple arrangements exist. These multiple elements are combined into one revenue accounting contract for allocation and recognition purposes. Such combined contracts are called "multiple element arrangements."

The combination of multiple elements into one revenue accounting contract can be performed:

- When processing of the revenue accounting items takes place,
- Manually, after multiple contracts have been created.

3.4.6.1 Combination of RAIs into one revenue accounting contract

Revenue Accounting Items which share common attributes can be combined into one revenue accounting contract during the RAI processing. For example, all RAIs created for the same customer in the same currency, including information from different upstream processes (e.g. different sales order types in SD), can be combined into one revenue accounting contract.

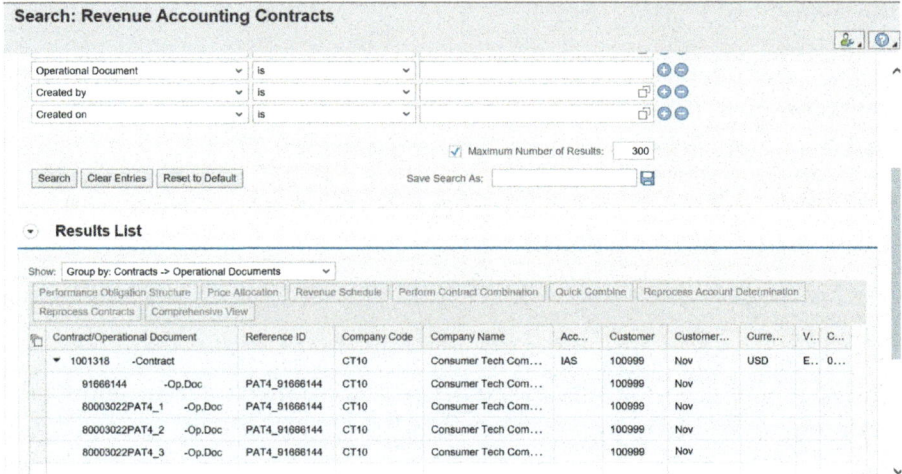

Figure 56   SAP RAR: Combined contract

After a user creates a combined contract, any relevant changes to sales orders combined into the contract will lead to the creation of changed RAIs. After RAI processing, the changed RAIs will be updated in the combined contract. Additionally, if new sales orders are created with parameters that match the contract combination criteria, then the data will be included into the already existing combined contract during RAI processing.

The logic for this type of contract combination is provided within a BAdI. The minimum requirements in SAP Revenue Accounting and Reporting for contract combination are:

1. The same company code,
2. The same currency,
3. The same sold-to party.

Using the BAdI, customers can implement additional requirements for contract combination, such as the distribution channel (e.g. business unit). If set this way, a combination will only take place if the distribution channels of the data to be processed are the same.

3.4.6.2 Manual combination of contracts

Whenever automated contract combination is not in use or has not been performed, manual contract combination can be applied. Manual combination follows the same minimum combination requirements as automated combination during RAI processing:

1. The same company code,
2. The same currency,
3. The same sold-to party.

Manual contract combination is performed after contract creation. At that point, users can decide which elements and/or contracts shall be combined or deleted.

There are two ways contracts can be combined manually:

1. With **quick-combine functionality**. This option allows users to select two contracts and to execute contract combination without manually moving POBs from one to another contract. The effects of the contract combination (e.g. allocation effects of a combined contract) will only be visible after the combination is complete.

   If a user selects the quick combine functionality, only one contract will remain after the combination is performed. The POBs from all other contracts will be copied into that one contract, and the remaining contracts without POBs will be removed automatically. The user decides which contract number to over-take and retain.

   The quick-combine functionality is used to avoid having to check the results of an allocation or select specific POBs to include.

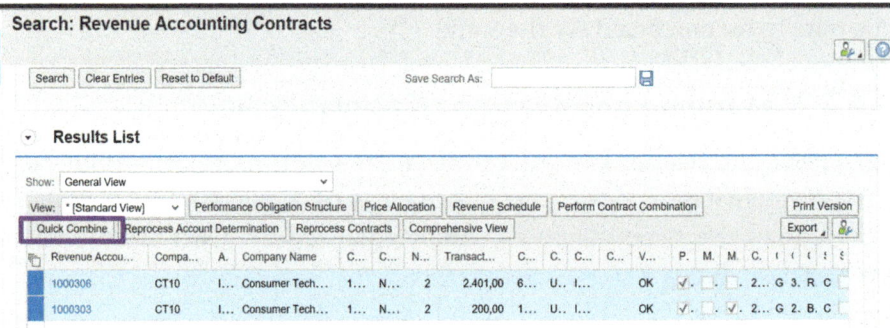

Figure 57   SAP RAR: Quick combine option

2. With **fully manual contract combination**. This option offers extended functionalities for contract combination. Users can precisely control which POBs of a contract should be copied over to the combined contract. In addition, users get an overview of the allocations after contract combination and before final acceptance of the contract.

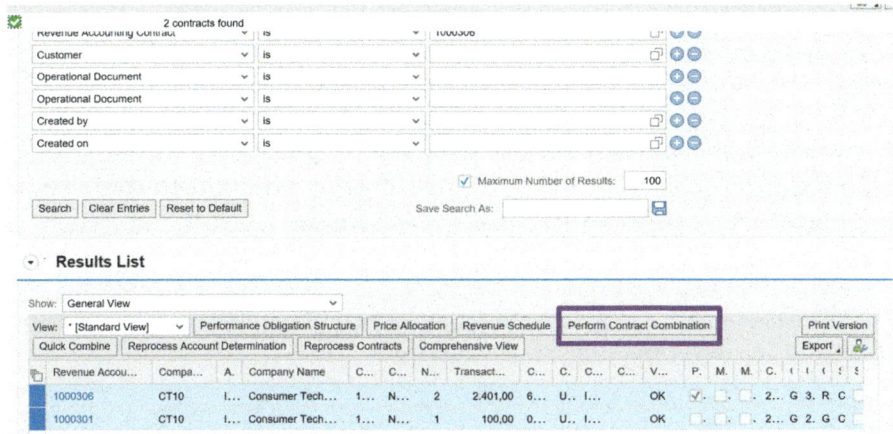

Figure 58   SAP RAR: Perform contract combination

3.4.6.3 Restrictions for contract combination

The contract combination logic has some restrictions which are equally applicable for automatic contract combination during RAI processing as well as for manual contract combination.

Restrictions include:

- Data/existing contracts from different company codes cannot be combined,
- Data/existing contracts for different customers cannot be combined,
- Data/existing contracts with different currencies cannot be combined.

For manual contract combination (quick combine or fully manual combination), the following restrictions apply:

- Contracts can be combined as long as only one contract has postings. POBs from contracts with postings cannot be moved to the contract without postings. However, it is possible to move unposted POBs to a contract with posted POBs,
- Contract combination will not be allowed if both contracts have invoiced amounts in revenue accounting.

These restrictions apply only to manual combination because in that case, a revenue accounting contract is already created before any combination takes place.

For example, if order and invoice RAIs will be processed, then a contract with the invoiced amount will be created. If a user attempts to combine this contract with another contract that has an invoiced amount, the system will block the step.

On the other hand, the automated contract combination takes place during RAI processing and the following happens:

1. First, the system will identify that order and invoice RAIs should be combined into an existing contract with an invoice amount,

2. Second, order RAIs will be processed and information will be assigned to the desired revenue accounting contract,

3. Finally, invoice RAIs will be processed. These invoice RAIs will update invoiced amounts on the existing combined contract.

3.5 Conflict handling

Sometimes conflicts result when the data received from the operational application through RAI processing does not match the values in the revenue accounting module that were changed manually. For instance, a conflict will occur if allocation was changed manually based on a contract value of 890 euros, but later the 890 euros became 925 euros.

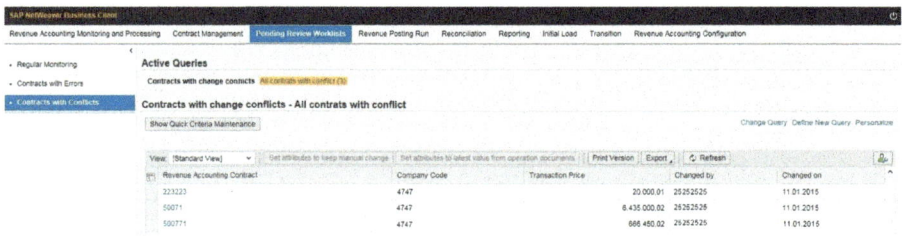

Figure 59   SAP RAR: Contracts with conflict worklist

Contracts in conflict are automatically excluded from the revenue posting run. In order to solve the conflict, users need to check the conflict details and manually resolve the conflict. Typically, users compare contract values before the changes were received with those after the change and decide which value to keep in the contract.

Conflicts can be created in the following areas:

- **Attributes**: An attribute of the POB is changed manually and the SD order gets updated. Conflict on POB attributes are recorded, such as a conflict because of changes to the start and/or end dates.
- **Price allocation**: A conflict will occur when price allocation is manually changed in a revenue accounting contract and then subsequent changes are made to input values on the linked sales order. This happens, for instance, when another line item is added that increases the value of the contract.

  In this case, the manual allocation is overwritten by the new values and the system will automatically allocate the price using the latest contractual price. However, the system will "remember" the allocation amounts before changes, and it will indicate that a change took place. Users can still decide to keep unchanged price allocations for some of the performance obligations but not the overall allocation of the contract, if a contractual price was changed.
- **Spreading:** Manual spreading is changed for a time-based performance obligation in a contract. Subsequently, the allocated amount for the same performance obligation is changed. In this case, the manual spreading will be overwritten using the new allocation price, and a conflict will be created. The system will record the values before the change and after the change. Users can manually adjust spreading values by re-entering the old values again, however, if a new allocation price is used, it is not possible to keep all of the old spreading because the sum of the spreading will not match the new allocated amount.
- **Add/deleted POB:** The contract is changed manually, for example, price allocation is adjusted manually. Subsequently, another performance obligation is added or deleted for the same contract. A conflict entry will be created in the conflict list.

As mentioned, when the operational document (e.g. the sales order in the SAP Sales and Distribution module) sends an update to the revenue accounting contract, changes are always applied to the contract and its POBs. This means that if you open the revenue contract, you will always see the latest value from the operational documents. However, at the same time, the contract will be put to conflict status. This will block the entire contract from revenue postings as long as conflicts within the contract are not resolved. Such a conflict is only marked in revenue accounting and does not impact the sender component and processes like delivery, goods issue, invoicing etc.

Below is an example of the conflict handling functionality:

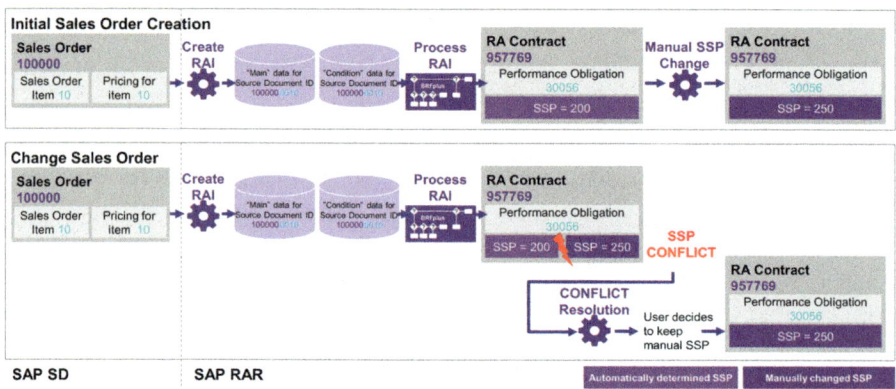

Figure 60   Example of a conflict caused through manual Stand-alone Selling Price (SSP) changes

When the POB was initially created, the stand-alone selling price (SSP) was 200.

A user manually changes the SSP from 200 to 250 in revenue accounting.

When the operational document changes the SSP from 200 (based on previous operational data) to 220, and these changes are processed to revenue accounting, a change in the SSP field in revenue accounting is detected. Hereby, revenue accounting will compare the latest value from the operational document (220) with the manually changed value (250). This causes a conflict in the SSP field to be recorded, since the latest value from the operational system is different from the value that was changed manually. As a result, the contract will be put to the conflict list for review.

3.5.1 Settings in conflict handling

In order to adjust conflict handling to individual company needs, SAP Revenue Accounting and Reporting offers three options for handling conflicts in the master data fields for performance obligations, such as SSPs, start and end data, and descriptions.

These settings are applied for a company code or in general for all company codes within the SAP client. In addition, every single POB can have its own settings which are applicable for the entire lifetime of the performance obligation and will supersede the customizing settings on the company code or SAP client level. Following is a description of the three settings:

1. **Always check conflicts:** This is the default update mode. Revenue accounting will always check whether there is a conflict on an attribute (e.g. a POB field) when the operational document is updated with a value other than the manually changed value in the revenue accounting contract.

2. **Always keep manual changes:** In case this option is activated, POB attributes that are manually changed will not be overwritten through updates from operational applications. Please note, as mentioned above, this and other conflict handling options are only relevant for POB attributes. As such, it will not prevent price allocation or spreading conflicts caused through price changes/or changes to the contractual value. On the contrary, conflicts must be recorded whenever a price change occurs, since net values from the sender component (e.g. SAP SD) must be equal to the value of a contract.

3. **Always overwrite automatically:** When the operational document sends a new value, the manually changed POB fields will be automatically overwritten by incoming changes. Conflicts will not be created for the fields with this setting, e.g. manual SSP changes will always be overwritten by data received from the sender component.

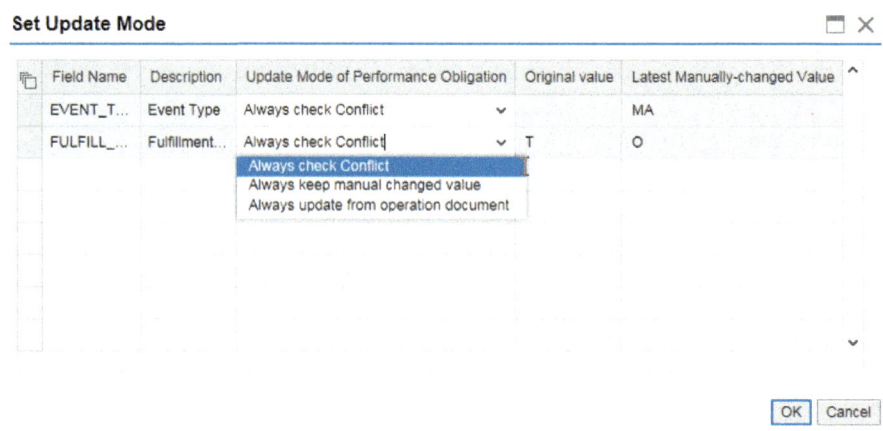

Figure 61   SAP RAR: Update modes for Performance Obligations

3.5.2 Contracts in conflict worklist

As discussed previously and shown in Figure 59 all contracts with conflicts are automatically included in the worklist "Contracts with Conflicts".

Any contracts in this worklist require manual conflict resolution. The user has to open the worklist and start reviewing and solving the conflicts. After a conflict is resolved, it will be removed from the conflict worklist and the revenue can be recognized.

In order to organize conflict handling, the conflict worklist includes the following categories:

- Conflicts in revenue accounting attributes Within this category, all contracts with conflicts in POB master data fields are displayed,
- Price allocation conflicts,
- Revenue scheduling (or revenue spreading) conflicts,
- Conflicts because of added or deleted performance obligations.

Every category provides an overview of manually changed values and newly received changes after RAI processing.

To avoid a large number of contracts with conflicts and to improve the automation of revenue accounting processes, we recommend avoiding unnecessary changes in the revenue accounting module. If changes are required and possible, it's best to perform them directly in the sender component. We also recommend closely monitoring the conflict worklist to ensure quick resolution so that posting can be completed.

3.6 Error handling

SAP Revenue Accounting and Reporting includes a special worklist for contracts with errors.

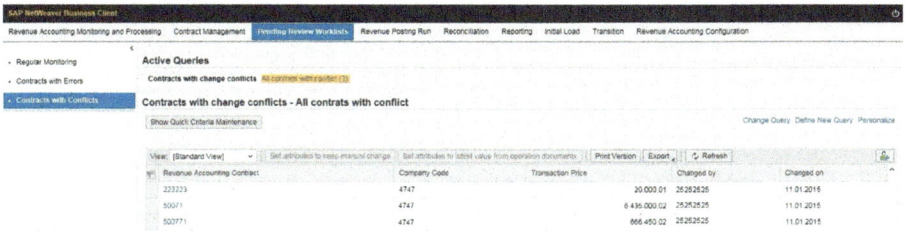

Figure 62   SAP RAR: Contracts with errors worklist

An error is different than a conflict. A conflict happens when data is manually changed by a user within the revenue accounting contract and that later conflicts with an update received from a sender component.

An error, on the other hand, prevents further processing because of inconsistency in the performance obligation data or a contract. Contracts in the error status won't be posted and can only be changed (ideally in the sender component) to resolve the errors.

Typically, errors are related to performance obligation attributes/fields. A few examples of such errors are:

- The start and/or end date of a performance obligation is missing,
- The stand-alone selling price is missing,
- A revenue account cannot be derived for a performance obligation.

In most cases, errors happen because of the configuration in the BRFplus. During RAI processing, a number of checks are executed to help users avoid creating contracts and performance obligations that result in errors. However, errors can also occur when current performance obligation attributes are no longer valid after the configuration has been changed.

In order to monitor contracts in the error status, a special worklist is used. This worklist includes all contracts with errors and helps users navigate to the detail level to understand the problem. Issues can be solved manually through user input or might require changes in customizing or the BRFplus configuration. In some cases, to solve an issue, changes in operational data (e.g. sales orders) and subsequent RAI processing would be required.

As mentioned before, contracts with error status are excluded from any further processing in revenue accounting (including posting) until the errors are resolved. Hence, it is important to ensure that the error worklist is monitored regularly and issues are resolved well in advance of period-end closing.

3.7 Revenue posting process

The fifth and final step in the IFRS 15 revenue recognition model applies to fulfilled performance obligations.

In the SAP Revenue Accounting and Reporting module, this process is split into three steps as follows:

1. Calculation of time-based revenues.
2. Results of the calculation are stored within a posting table. Calculation of liabilities and assets.

   This step applies to deferred and unbilled revenues. Results of these calculation steps are recorded in a posting table.
3. Revenue posting run.
   This is the final step which transfers the data from the posting table to the accounting interface to create financial postings.

3.7.1 Processing of Revenue Accounting Items

A prerequisite for any of the activities in the revenue accounting module is processing of the Revenue Accounting Items (RAI). RAIs need to be processed to ensure that the latest updates from the sender component are included in the revenue posting process. Otherwise, potentially important information might be excluded from the posting execution process.

We recommend ensuring well in advance that RAIs are processed and potential RAI processing errors are solved or at least known, so that they can be accounted for properly and in time.

For more on RAI processing, please refer to Chapter 3.3.3.

3.7.2 Prepare contracts for posting

Once the RAIs are processed, revenue accounting users can start to verify the contracts and their respective POBs, or modify the contracts if necessary. This step is important so that users will know which contracts and POBs are going to be considered for revenue posting.

POBs may not be considered for posting for one of the following reasons:

- A POB is suspended from revenue posting because it must be reviewed. For example, the revenue accounting tool can be setup so that all newly created POBs will be assigned a specific reason for review. This means POBs are suspended from revenue posting until they are reviewed.

- A POB is suspended from revenue posting because of a conflict (e.g. a price allocation conflict). No revenue posting lines in posting table will be created for POBs in the conflict status. The user has to solve the conflict to make sure that the POB is posted with the next posting run.

- A POB is in error status. Posting of the POB cannot take place due to the error, such as an error from an asset or liability calculation. Users must resolve the error before posting is possible.

3.7.3 Posting table

As indicated in previous chapters, the posting table plays a central role in the posting process. FI documents are created out of the data available in the posting table.

The posting table contains all posting-relevant information for periods when posting has already taken place.

In addition, the posting table contains all entries for the actual revenue accounting period in which:

- A time-based calculation has occurred,
- A liabilities and asset calculation has occurred,
- Manual fulfillment or a fulfillment event has occurred.
- Manual fulfillments were executed directly in the revenue accounting module for percentage of completion. POBs are immediately recorded into the posting table if the affected POBs were not suspended,
- An event took place (e.g. a customer event invoice resulted in an immediate record in the posting table), and the related POB was not suspended,
- Invoice RAIs were processed. (Invoice RAIs create an invoice correction entry in the posting table immediately after processing without errors).

The main purpose of the posting table is to prepare the data for FI postings. The table contains all credit and debit lines with corresponding amounts and currencies, as well as gain and loss account numbers to be used for FI posting. All entries on the table are categorized to indicate the type of posting to be performed. The posting categories are:

- Contract Liability,
- Contract Asset,
- Receivable Adjustment,
- Revenue,
- Cost Correction,
- Deferred Revenue,
- Unbilled Receivable,
- Invoice Correction,
- Cost,
- Cost Adjustment,
- Exchange Rate Differences,
- Statistic,

- Refund Liability,
- Refund Asset.

3.7.4 Execute posting

The posting process in SAP RAR is divided into 3 steps:

1. Time-based calculations

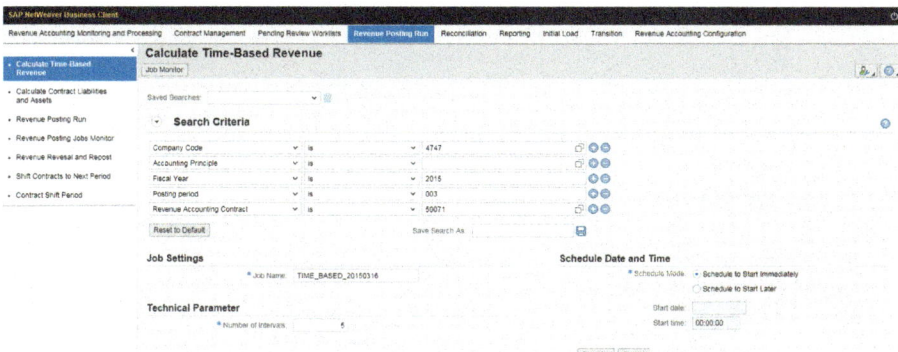

Figure 63   SAP RAR: Calculate time-based revenue

2. Liabilities and assets calculations

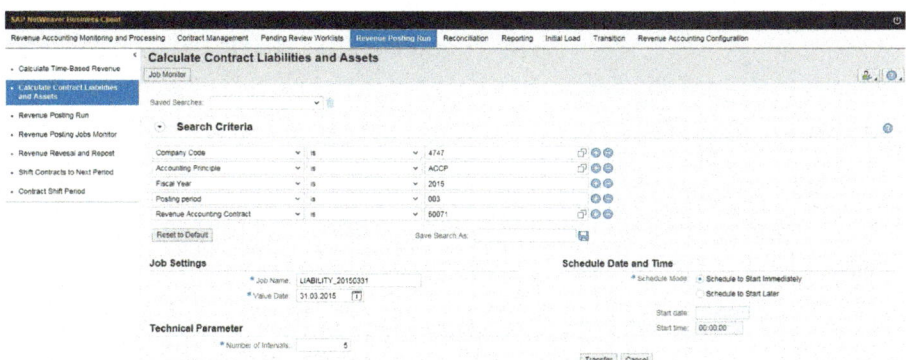

Figure 64   SAP RAR: Calculate contract liabilities and assets

3. Posting runs

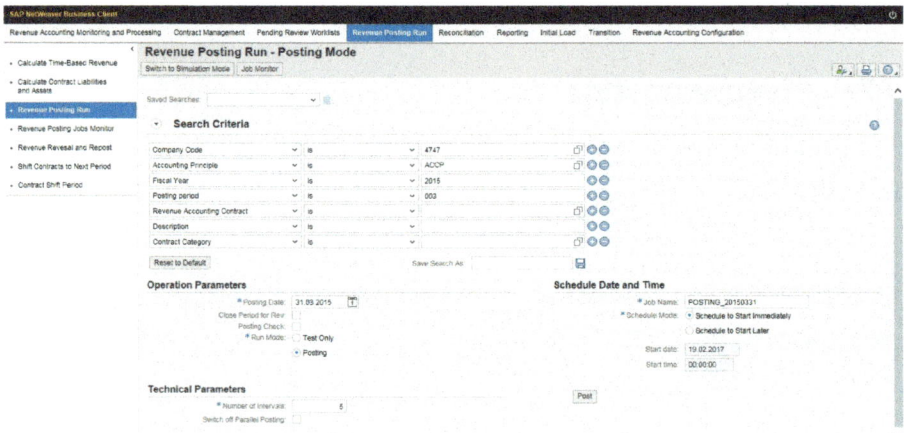

Figure 65   SAP RAR: Execute revenue posting run

A user needs to execute three programs to complete the above-mentioned steps.

When doing a posting run, it's important to follow the steps precisely and in the order listed above. Otherwise, Step 3 will not include all relevant data for the current month. For example, if Step 1 is not performed, then no time-based revenue will be available for posting.

The same goes for the calculation of liabilities and assets – if the second step of the posting process is not completed, then assets and liabilities will not be available in the posting table.

If a user tries to perform a posting run without having completed Step 1 and Step 2, only those entries which were recorded after invoice RAI processing, manual fulfillment or event-based fulfillment for POBs will be included.

Please note, it is not possible to close a period without performing Step 1 and Step 2 for all contracts which have some entries in the posting table. An error message will be displayed that says that one or both steps are required to close a period in revenue accounting.

3.7.4.1 Posting runs executed prior to period-end closing

All three steps can be scheduled to run periodically based on organizational requirements. The posting runs will record a financial posting (if all three posting steps are performed). By running regular postings before the final closing of a month, financial postings (FI documents) are created. If no changes are made to the contracts which were already posted, then the final run will only "flag" the period as closed.

In other words, this means that the runtime for postings at period end is shortened since the posting was already created in advance.

Organizations with large numbers of revenue accounting contracts should consider running posting jobs before closing posting, since this helps to reduce closing time.

It is important to mention that Steps 1, 2 and 3 (if not executed with a closing option) can be used for individual contracts or contract ranges and categories. This allows flexibility for posting run executions before period closings.

3.7.4.2 Final posting run – period-end closing

Period-end closing posting runs are executed in accordance with the financial period closing calendar.

SAP Revenue Accounting and Reporting posts to the financial accounts of an organization, which means that the closing posting must follow the financial closing calendar. If it doesn't, the system would try to record the postings in the closed period and will fail.

In Revenue Accounting and Reporting, closing means that the last open reconciliation key (an object which typically stands for a period of one month, but can also be customized, e.g. for a quarterly closing cycle) of a current period will be closed and no further changes to the closed reconciliation key will be allowed. The current open period in Revenue Accounting is then changed to the next month.

The closing process is always executed for all contracts of a company code and can never be executed for individual contracts.

Period-end closing in revenue accounting will not take place if:

1. **Time-based calculation is not executed:** This step must be executed for all contracts in which POBs are not suspended from revenue posting.

2. **Liabilities and asset calculations are not executed:** This step must be executed for all contracts in which POBs are not suspended from revenue posting.

In other words, if for one or more contracts, Steps 1 and 2 of the posting run process were not executed, the whole period in revenue accounting will not be closed. The user would first have to execute Steps 1 and 2 prior to running a closing posting run.

We recommend executing closing postings one after another. Users can set a special status on a company-code level. Called the "In Closing" status, it makes sure any updates to contracts are automatically recorded to the next period (e.g. the reconciliation key of the next month). For example, while preparing closing activities for the third quarter, a user can set the status "In Closing" for a company code. If RAIs are changed, those changes will be automatically recorded to the first month of the fourth quarter.

This way, users do not have to execute time-based and/or liabilities and asset calculations prior to closing the period.

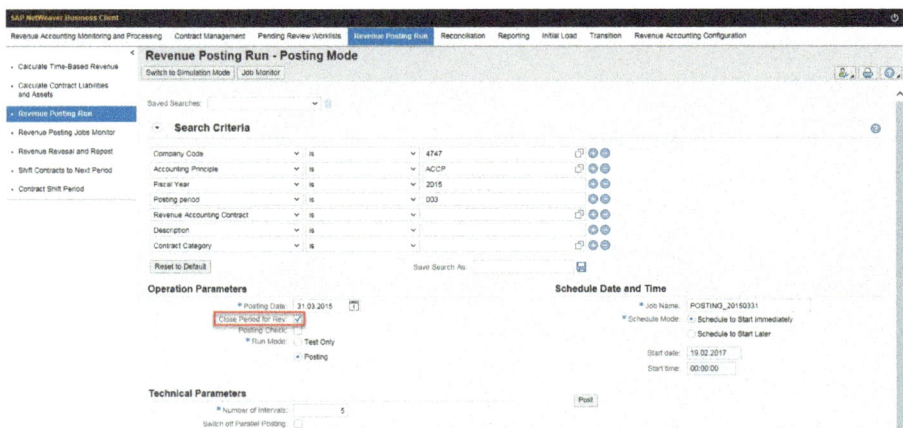

Figure 66   SAP RAR: Execute final posting run – Close period in revenue accounting

After a posting run is successfully executed at the end of a period, no more changes to the closed period are possible and the system automatically updates the period status as "closed".

3.8 Reconciliation and reporting capabilities

SAP Revenue Accounting and Reporting is equipped with a number of reconciliation and operational reports. It also includes ready-to-use Data Sources for extracting information from revenue accounting tables into the reporting database and preparing it according to the requirements.

This chapter describes standard reconciliation/operational report capabilities and provides in sights on the reporting capabilities of SAP RAR.

3.8.1 Standard reconciliation reports

The SAP Revenue Accounting and Reporting solution provides a number of ready-to-use reconciliation reports. Within this chapter, we will describe selected reconciliation reports created to address business and technical reconciliation needs.

Reconciliation reports created for business users address the needs of particular users, such as revenue accountants that need to reconcile data planned to be posted by Revenue Accounting and data actually posted into the general ledger.

Technical reconciliation reports are provided to identify several types of differences linked to root causes of a technical nature. For example, such reports are used to check if all data available in the Revenue Accounting Items of a sender component is correctly processed into revenue accounting.

Standard reconciliation reports do not cover all potential business needs. For example, a ready-to-use report for reconciliation between revenue accounting and CO-PA is not provided. Depending on the reporting requirements, such a report can be created in the operational system or DataSources provided by SAP RAR can be used to satisfy the requirements in SAP Business Warehouse (BW).

3.8.1.1 G/L Accounts between Revenue Accounting and General Ledger

This report can be used to show differences between the planned postings for accounts used in revenue accounting and actual postings made to the same accounts in the general ledger. Using red and green traffic light symbols, the report helps the user to easily detect accounts with differences between revenue accounting and the general ledger. Yet the displayed differences do not necessarily mean that an error occurred during posting. It is possible that manual journal entries were performed to an account. In order to understand the details, users must check the posting details and history.

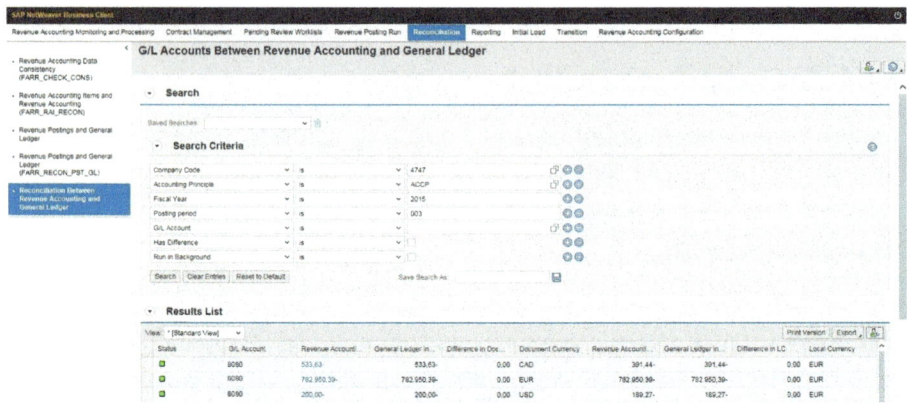

Figure 67   SAP RAR: Selection criteria and results of report "G/L accounts between Revenue Accounting and General Ledger"

3.8.1.2 FI documents and revenue accounting contracts

This report is used to explain which performance obligations and contracts have been posted. It provides a link between these elements and the general ledger-posting document. Therefore, after posting a run execution, users can clearly see a link between performance obligation/revenue accounting contracts and the general ledger posting document. "FI documents", or financial accounting documents, and revenue accounting contract reports do not identify/display any type of differences.

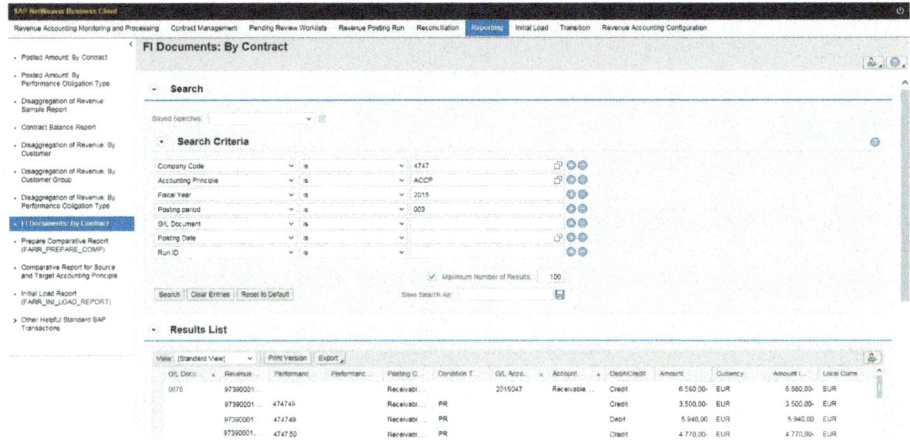

Figure 68   SAP RAR: Selection criteria and results of report "FI Documents: By Contract"

3.8.1.3 Reconciliation between revenue posting and general ledger

The target audience for this report is technical users. This report compares data prepared for posting (data from the posting table) to data posted during the posting run. The reconciliation can be executed based on the unique posting run ID. This enables a precise comparison between the "planned" posting data from the posting table and the "actual" posted data in the general ledger.

Differences identified by this report are most likely caused by technical issues. Analysis of the data needs to be performed by technically skilled users to identify the root causes of errors. Typically, such a report should be executed as a part of closing activities before the periods are finally closed. This allows users to identify wrong postings and correct them on time. If it is not done in time, corrections must be done in the next month in revenue accounting. Alternatively, users can correct the items with manual journal entries.

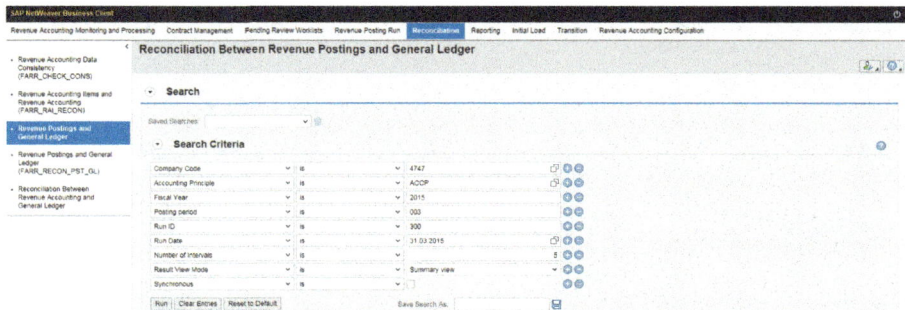

Figure 69   SAP RAR: Selection criteria of report "Reconciliation between Revenue Posting and General Ledger"

3.8.1.4 Reconciliation of Revenue Accounting Items with contracts

Another technical report provided by SAP Revenue Accounting and Reporting is Reconciliation of Revenue Accounting Items with contracts. The aim of this report is to enable reconciliation between Revenue Accounting Items (RAIs) and revenue accounting performance obligations and contracts. It compares information available in the RAIs against the data in performance obligation and contracts. Every sender component (e.g. SAP Sales and Distribution) records all operational changes relevant for revenue accounting in RAIs. Processing of these RAIs ensures that the information is transferred into the revenue accounting elements – e.g. performance obligation and revenue accounting contracts.

In case data requested to be transferred to revenue accounting (processed RAIs) does not match the data actually available, the report will show the differences. For example, the report can detect the following differences:

- Difference in price and cost of an item. Hereby prices and costs from processed RAIs are compared against the same parameters in the revenue accounting performance obligation. If different pricing conditions are used for the sales order and invoice, then reconciliation, including transaction price adjustments of a POB through invoice updates, is not possible.

- Difference in total invoice amount of a performance obligation. Here total invoiced amount of a POB is compared to the total invoice amount of corresponding item line from the sender component.

- Difference in invoiced amount (price and cost) per condition type. Here the conditions of processed invoice RAIs are compared to the conditions of a POB in revenue accounting.

- Difference in fulfilled quantity. This check is based on a comparison of an RAI's fulfilled quantity versus fulfilled quantities of a POB. POBs for which fulfillment event and fulfillment type have been changed – meaning comparison of the quantities cannot be performed – are flagged on the report output list.

- Difference in recognized cost. This report compares the amount of recognized costs from processed RAIs to the values in corresponding POBs.

This report needs to be verified by technically skilled users to find out where and how the corrections need to be applied – for example, if possible, by re-sending a set of changed RAIs to adjust the data in the revenue accounting contract/performance obligation. If applicable, manual adjustments of the contract data in revenue accounting can be applied to correct the difference.

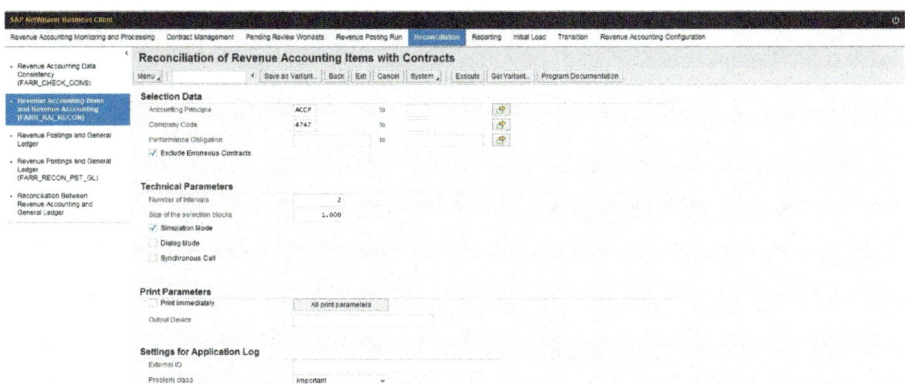

Figure 70   SAP RAR: Selection criteria of report "Reconciliation of Revenue Accounting Items with Contracts"

3.8.2 Reporting – SAP's DataSources for legal reporting and analytics

IFRS 15 includes specific requirements designed to improve revenue recognition disclosures. According to IFRS 15, an entity should disclose sufficient information to enable users of financial statements to understand the nature, amount, timing and uncertainty of revenue and cash flows arising from contracts with customers.

The specific disclosure requirements for contracts with customers are:

- Disaggregation of revenue – IFRS 15 says entities must split/disaggregate the revenue intothe following categories:
  o Geographical,
  o Contract type,
  o Business units,
  o Service type.
- Transparency in the way contract balances are disclosed. The following should be disclosed:
  o Opening and closing balances of receivables, contract assets and liabilities,
  o Revenue recognized in the reporting period that was included in the contract liability balance at the beginning of the period,
  o Revenue recognized in the reporting period from performance obligations fully or partially fulfilled in previous periods (e.g. because of transaction price changes),
  o Disclosure of performance obligation details. An example is: When the fulfillment of the POB has taken place, what are the payment terms, type of goods or services, returns and warranty obligations? In addition, IFRS 15 requires entities to provide an aggregated amount for the transaction price that is allocated to POBs, even if they have not yet been fulfilled and the final amount cannot be predicted.

Management reporting needs are typically satisfied with the use of reporting applications like SAP Business Warehouse (BW). Here it is important to ensure that sufficient data from the source system is provided. The reports are built in the reporting application.

To enable both legal and management reports, SAP Revenue Accounting and Reporting provides DataSources. DataSources represent a collection/set of fields with data to be transferred into the BW application.

To utilize the DataSources, customers have to deliver their own BW content. The DataSources can be used on both conventional databases and HANA.

The advantage of DataSources is that they provide direct database table access to all relevant information for revenue accounting on a granular level. Customers have predefined data extractors from the revenue accounting application and only need to design the presentation logic of the reports in BW.

For transaction data, three primary DataSources are available:

DataSource	Description	Details
0FARR_RA_10	Revenue Analysis by Posting Item	Posted revenue by category (e.g. revenue, contract liability)
0FARR_RA_20	Allocated Price Change of POB	Allocation amount changes per POB per period
0FARR_RA_30	Revenue Forecast	Revenue planned / forecasted to be recognized in the future

Figure 71   Standard SAP Revenue Accounting and Reporting DataSources –
Transaction DataSources

Additionally, DataSources for master data and texts are provided:

DataSource	Description
0FARR_OBJNR_ATTR	Revenue object attribute
0FARR_CONTRACT_ATTR	Revenue contract attributes
0FARR_POB_ATTR	POB attributes
0FARR_RECKEY_ATTR	Reconciliation key attributes
0FARR_RECKEY_STAT_TEXT	Reconciliation key status text
0FARR_CONTR_CAT_TEXT	Contract category text
0FARR_EVT_TYPE_TEXT	Event type text
0FARR_POB_TYPE_TEXT	POB text type
0FARR_FULFILL_TYPE_TEXT	Fulfillment type text
0FARR_POB_ROLE_TEXT	POB role text
0FARR_POB_STAT_TEXT	POB status text
0FARR_POST_CAT_TEXT	Posting category text
0FARR_ST_DAT_TYP_TEXT	Start date type text
0FARR_DIST_TYP_TEXT	Distinct type text
0FARR_DEF_S_IND_TEXT	POB special indicator text
0FARR_REV_RSN_TEXT	Review reason text
0FARR_VAL_RES_TEXT	Validation result text

Figure 72   Standard SAP Revenue Accounting and Reporting DataSources – Data-
Sources for attributes and text descriptions

Implementation of SAP Revenue Accounting and Reporting

When SAP RAR is implemented, it includes a framework to meet regulatory requirements. The standard version of SAP RAR was designed to work with different accounting principles like IFRS 15.

The complexity of an SAP Revenue Accounting and Reporting implementation depends on regulatory and business requirements. Business requirements may include adaptations for specific practices and processes, including a migration from existing revenue accounting solutions to SAP Revenue Accounting and Reporting.

Given the regulatory and business-specific requirements of implementing SAP RAR, companies need to:

- Adapt business and IT processes to the new regulations in the revenue accounting and reporting standard,
- Adapt/customize the standard SAP Revenue Accounting and Reporting solution to meet specific business requirements.

4.1 Implementation approach

As described in the previous chapters, SAP Revenue Accounting and Reporting receives and consumes data from applications with operational data, such as the SAP Sales and Distribution Module. Information about transactions with customers is transferred into the revenue accounting module and processed in accordance to regulatory, legal and customer-specific requirements. The goal is to enable accurate revenue reporting.

Obviously, implementation of SAP RAR is highly dependent on upstream processes. This dependency is not purely dictated by existing IT architecture; business processes also make a big difference, since they are impacted by

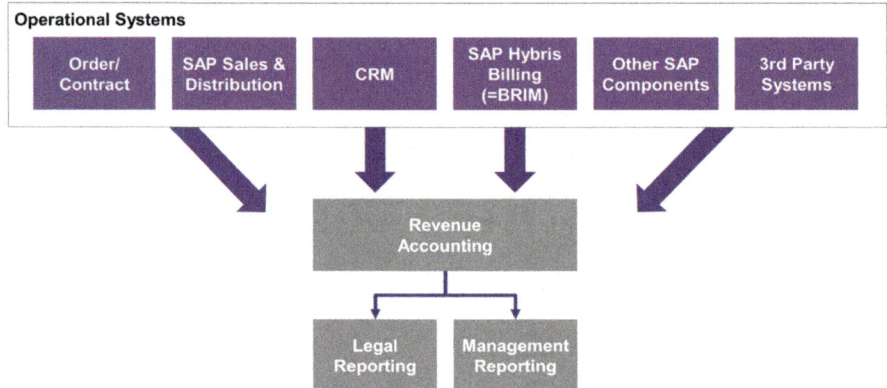

Figure 73   DataSources and reporting requirements impacting SAP RAR implementation

the implementation of the new revenue accounting standard and by a new software component.

For these reasons, it's critical to conduct an analysis of end-to-end processes that may be affected. Specifically, for a software implementation, the analysis needs to include:

- **Revenue reporting-relevant information sources, data and process flows:** The goal is to identify all sources of revenue-relevant information and understand current data flows as well as identify all relevant interfaces (inbound and outbound).

    Process flows will provide transparency for the whole business process, and the analysis should include a mapping roles and responsibilities of involved parties.

- **Analysis of period-end closing procedures:** An analysis of existing period-end closing procedures is important for understanding the impact and dependencies of an SAP RAR implementation.

- **Regulatory and audit requirements:** Understanding regulatory and audit requirements is critical for an SAP RAR implementation. These requirements describe the way data will be consumed and processed in SAP RAR.

- **Legal and Management Reporting requirements:** Defining these reporting requirements is important for understanding which information needs to be stored and extracted from SAP RAR to prepare reports.
- **Customer-specific and/or industry requirements:** It's important to know how customer and/or industry requirements will impact SAP RAR and to understand specific regulatory and legal requirements.

Comprehensive analysis of the processes should be seen as a prerequisite for a SAP Revenue Accounting and Reporting implementation. The more details that can be gathered during the process analysis, the better the solution that will be provided. This is critical for SAP RAR implementations, since revenue accounting is a downstream process which consumes data from other applications. The implementation team must ensure that the required data will be provided in the proper quality.

Analysis of the revenue accounting-relevant and dependent processes can start independently of actual SAP RAR implementation efforts. In many industries and business, analysis of the existing processes will be conducted anyway to match existing business practices to IFRS 15. A key for successful SAP RAR implementation is to align efforts on the business side with IT. Business processes are the first to be impacted by the implementation of a new revenue recognition standard. Software comes next.

Once the impact of IFRS 15 to existing business processes is understood, IT processes outside revenue accounting need to be reviewed for possible adjustment. For example, recording and processing contracts with customers might need review to stay compliant with IFRS 15. To effectively implement and run SAP Revenue Accounting and Reporting, companies need to evaluate if they must adapt upstream processes. To do this, IT specialists from outside revenue accounting are required.

The implementation of SAP RAR affects multiple areas of a company. To manage the transition, business and IT experts within each area of the company should be involved in the implementation, since even long-standing business processes might have to be changed.

In addition, auditors should be involved in the implementation process to advise and approve any potential process changes.

Pitfalls during SAP RAR implementation include "silo" thinking and misunderstandings. Silo thinking happens when people believe the impact of an implementation is only downstream – e.g. on financial reporting. They believe that operational processes which deliver the data to revenue accounting will largely stay unchanged. And misunderstandings can happen when financial department clerks who use SAP RAR expect they can make changes to the data based on their needs, ignoring the fact that conflicts will occur within SAP RAR. Not changing the mindset described typically leads to problems in operations. A SAP RAR implementation affects a broad spectrum of business processes, starting from presales and sales, to financials, controlling and reporting. For successful implementation of SAP Revenue Accounting and Reporting, companies must ensure that all impacted parties are part of the implementation efforts.

Applying the proper change-management methodology will help to avoid pitfalls and misunderstandings. The change management team must explain the end-to-end business processes and their consequences after SAP RAR is implemented.

Automation is another important aspect to be considered during SAP RAR implementation. As described in the previous chapters, SAP Revenue Accounting and Reporting provides a set of tools and functions to achieve a high level of automation for revenue accounting processes. However, its automation capabilities may not be effectively used if existing processes are not adapted (e.g. order and billing management). To benefit from the automation features, existing operational upstream processes need to be analyzed and, if required, adapted. In addition, based on the analysis, the implementation team needs to decide how to customize settings and implement custom coding within the revenue accounting module. It's important to fully align upstream processes and IT supported functionalities with revenue accounting requirements to avoid unnecessary manual adjustments and steps.

4.2 Migration activities

Data migration in SAP Revenue Accounting and Reporting is the transfer of all relevant data into SAP RAR from applications previously used. In this step, all contracts with customers that may require modification after the transfer should be part of the migration.

The migration process requires operational data and legacy data to be transferred into SAP RAR.

- Operational data is data from contracts with customers. For example, if SAP RAR is integrated with SAP SD, the sales orders and invoicing documents are considered operational data.
- Legacy data includes information about revenue recognized prior to migration.

Both operational and legacy data are required by the migration team to create contracts and performance obligations in SAP RAR. Legacy data includes recognized revenue from the past, and operational data includes invoices created in the past. In addition, any revenues to be recognized in the future must also be considered.

Operational data is also used to create revenue accounting objects like contracts and performance obligations.

For all migrated contracts, information about the revenue recognized in the past and past invoicing is collected during the migration period.

Data collected within this period will never be posted to the general ledger by SAP RAR and cannot be changed, since it represents data already posted from all past periods.

But this information is important for calculating open revenue to be recognized after migration, as well as respective liabilities and assets.

To define the migration period, the migration team must select a date range for migration activities. When the period is over, revenue recognition and reporting, as well as postings, will start in SAP RAR. All events and postings that took place before this date will be added up and recorded in the migration period. The migration period is displayed on the revenue schedule of a migrated contract. The total contractual value, invoiced amount, and recognized amount of every migrated contract includes values from migration and periods after migration.

To start the migration into SAP RAR, a migration period needs to be defined. This means the transfer date needs to be set and the migration status/mode must be activated for the affected company code and defined data set (Migration Package). The reason for setting a migration status is to determine the system behavior during the loading of migration data and to enable the loading of data. As long as the migration mode is switched on, any events that happen but have an event date after the transfer date will not be processed into revenue accounting, since they are not related to the migration.

Migration into SAP Revenue Accounting and Reporting can be executed on the level of company code (e.g. the business organization unit within SAP), or more granularly, based on a combination of company code and migration package. Migration and subsequent validation of large data sets from one company code might take significant amounts of time. That is why SAP RAR allows users to define migration packages. The definition of migration packages and their assignment to Revenue Accounting Items (RAI) is defined in a BAdI. One migration package can include data from one or multiple company codes. For example, a migration package can include revenue accounting data of specific sales organizations and distribution channels for one or multiple company codes.

Before starting the migration in SAP RAR, the team must ensure that the migration period is closed in the application that contains legacy data for migration. This is mandatory to avoid changes in migration data.

The execution of the migration process in SAP Revenue Accounting and Reporting can be described as follows:

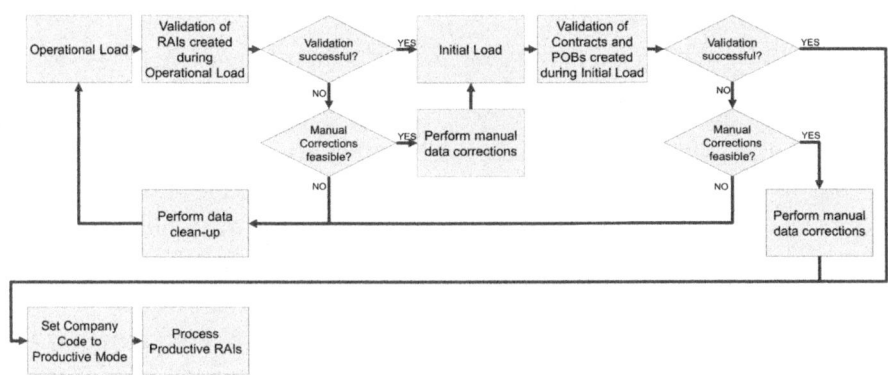

Figure 74   Migration process flow

1. **Operational Load:** During this step, all relevant revenue accounting data is taken from operational data and from legacy data (e.g. data that has already been recognized) and is used to create Revenue Accounting Items (RAI). During Operational Load, revenues that have already been recognized need to be sent to the special legacy data interface.

2. Once Operational Load is complete, the system creates Revenue Accounting Items that are marked to be processed through Initial Load. As stated before, this applies to all RAIs created with events that occur before the specified transfer date. Before proceeding with Initial Load, we recommend validating newly created RAIs to ensure that the first step was executed properly. This can be done with custom queries or reports.

3. If you need to correct a migrated RAI after Operational Load, you can do one of the following:

   a. Manually fix the affected RAIs. This approach is recommended only if minor changes are needed for a limited number of cases

   b. Delete the created RAIs and reload the corrected data. This approach can be used for individual and multiple RAIs and is recommended if the corrections needed are complex, or if corrections are needed for a large number of RAIs.

4. **Initial Load:** This step is used to process the RAIs created after operational data load. The result of this processing is revenue accounting contracts and performance obligations.

   To run Initial Load, the migration period in SAP RAR for all affected company codes must be closed.

   During Initial Load, all data is checked against the transfer date. Only data with a document date (similar to a creation date) before the transfer date is considered for processing during Initial Load. All other data is considered new operational data and will be processed after the migration is finished.

   All data that belongs to the period before the transfer date will be aggregated and assigned to the migration period.

   For example, Revenue Accounting Items with document dates before the transfer date, and end dates after the transfer date (document date < transfer date < end date), will be used for Initial Load processing. During the processing, data transferred through the legacy data interface (during Operational Load) will be considered. If both recognized revenue and the legacy invoice amounts have been provided, this information will be displayed during a special migration period for the newly created POB. In addition, if revenue schedules from the legacy system were migrated, then revenue spreading for the created POB after the migration period (e.g. after the transfer date) will be created for the provided data.

5. Once contracts and performance obligations are created, data validation steps are required. Such steps must include validation of the migrated legacy data – e.g. recognized revenues and invoiced amounts. If revenue schedules for periods after migration have been provided, those have to be validated as well. This type of validation must be done by IT, and it can require IT to create custom tools for validation.

   During Initial Load, recognized revenue and legacy invoiced amounts recorded within the migration period will also be recorded in the posting table. If recognized revenue and invoiced amounts per contract happen to be the same, no liabilities (unbilled amounts) and assets (deferred amounts) will be recorded during the migration period. However, if revenues are not equal to the invoices for a migrated contract, the implementation team must make sure that liabilities and assets are calculated for the migration period. Otherwise, the migration period will not include postings to balance the postings within the migration period. This means lines will be created in the next open period to balance liabilities and assets.

6. If you need to correct migrated data after Initial Load, you can:

   a. Fix data individually and manually. For example, after you validate migrated data, you will have a few points that need adjustment and can be corrected manually for a small number of items.

   b. Delete and reload. If recognized revenue or legacy invoice information was migrated incorrectly, or if large numbers of contracts need to be corrected, you can cleanup the migrated data and reload it (multiple or single contracts). After cleanup, you must repeat the Operational and Initial Load steps for all affected cases. Cleanup can only be done when the company code is in migration mode, and if the affected cases have not been posted to the general ledger.

7. After successful validation of migrated data, the company code has to be set to productive mode. This step marks the technical completion of migration activities.

8. Once company code has been set to productive mode, all RAIs which might have been created during migration need to be processed. As mentioned before, RAIs which are created during the migration process and have a start date and fulfillment event date after the transfer date, cannot be processed during migration.

    It's important to note that migration into SAP RAR does not impact ongoing operational processes, such as orders, deliveries, invoicing and modifications of these processes. Any potential order changes which occur after the Transfer Date will create RAIs which can only be processed after migration. Any returns, cancellations, credit memos, debit memos, and invoices created after the Transfer Date will not be considered part of the migration and would have to be processed after migration has been completed.

4.3 Testing SAP RAR

Testing plays a key role during implementation of SAP Revenue Accounting and Reporting. As mentioned, SAP RAR is a downstream application that receives data from operational data applications. This means that isolated testing of SAP RAR processes makes little sense, since the integration with applications that provide data for revenue accounting would not be tested along with them. The team should keep in mind that an integrated data flow will not necessarily work once the implementation is finished, if the system cannot be tested with data from upstream processes, such as the sales and billing modules.

Other important aspects of testing are to make sure that data from SAP RAR is correctly transferred to the general ledger, and controlling after the posting run is complete. Testing must include confirmation that financial and controlling data were recorded as expected after the revenue posting run.

The goal of SAP RAR testing is to ensure that:

- Integration with upstream processes works as expected and that all revenue accounting relevant information is received by SAP RAR,
- Processes within SAP RAR work as expected,
- SAP RAR delivers all required data in the expected quality to the general ledger, controlling and reporting.

This chapter will focus on specific SAP RAR testing aspects and will provide you with an overview on test preparation and execution. In addition, typical SAP RAR testing pitfalls will be highlighted.

4.3.1 Test preparation

Since a SAP RAR implementation affects multiple areas of a company, we recommend incorporating into your project plan enough time for test planning and preparation. Also, it's important to understand that tests must cover more than just processes within SAP RAR. Focusing only on SAP RAR requirements is a typical mistake.

Early on during test preparation, testing teams must understand end-to-end business scenarios which are relevant for revenue accounting. Typically, any revenue generating process of a company should be identified as a source of operational data for SAP RAR. These upstream processes should be executed to deliver input for SAP RAR testing during every test cycle, including unit, integration, user acceptance and regression testing.

Certainly, the scope of testing is SAP RAR, but you cannot test processes in SAP RAR without proper input of operational data.

Your test scenarios must include a good number of realistic scenarios. Consider scenarios where operational data might be changed. For example, after a sales order is created and RAIs are processed into revenue accounting, sales orders can still be changed. Those change scenarios need to be incorporated into the test. On top of all SAP RAR-specific modifications, like allocation and spreading changes, make sure to include all operational data changes into your test scenarios. If this is not done, it is likely that after go-live, some of the processes in the integrated environment will not function as expected.

Furthermore, SAP RAR test results should be validated to ensure that further downstream processes – such as controlling, finance and reporting – can consume the data provided by SAP RAR as expected.

All reports that rely on or consume SAP RAR data should be tested, since new reports may be created and existing reports may be modified during the implementation of SAP RAR.

For example, if SAP BW is used, the testing team must test the SAP BW reports that consume SAP RAR data. It is critical to validate that reports are accurate, since they are used for business decisions and reporting to external stakeholders, including authorities.

Since a typical SAP RAR implementation includes data migration, the project test team must also prepare testing for migration scenarios. We recommend to prepare migration testing in two stages:

1. The first stage should be used to test and validate migration data loads for SAP RAR,
2. The second stage is testing of migrated data (contracts) in SAP RAR.

One of the typical mistakes during migration testing is to test and validate only SAP RAR data migration. We strongly recommend that you test SAP RAR processes with migrated contracts. Make sure to test daily scenarios, based on migrated data, otherwise most common scenarios after SAP RAR go-live will remain untested. You will need to start data migration at an early stage to do this.

In addition, consider automating SAP RAR test execution. As mentioned, SAP RAR testing requires input from upstream processes and validation of test results in downstream applications. While planning your tests, check if test automation is already used for upstream or downstream processes.

If it is, incorporate test automation to significantly speed up test execution. Test automation in the SAP RAR module should be used for regression testing at the very least. However, test automation is also valuable for unit and integration testing. If you plan to use test automation, start preparing for it early in the project.

While preparing your tests, make sure you have enough skilled personnel for test execution, both from the IT and business departments. SAP RAR testing should be done with testing personnel from different areas of a company, to ensure that upstream data is provided properly and to test processes in downstream applications.

We recommend using a testing environment with a copy of real data, specifically if your migration is performed based on productive sales orders, deliveries and invoices. This way you can be prepared for SAP RAR data migration in the productive environment. Keep in mind that when using a copy of production data, you will need to consider matters of data privacy and data protection.

Basically, testing SAP RAR means testing end-to-end processes within a company. This is costly and time-consuming. However, without this effort, you face a high risk of problems with the system in the production environment. Consider this while planning and preparing for testing.

4.3.2 Test execution

In this chapter, we highlight the most critical topics to be considered during SAP RAR test execution. One of the most time-consuming tasks during SAP RAR test execution is coordination between different testing teams involved in end-to-end testing. To coordinate better, we recommend that experienced test managers are responsible for the test execution.

It is important to remember that the goal of test execution is to confirm that upstream processes are delivering the data for SAP RAR in the expected quality, that SAP RAR is able to receive and process that data, and that the output from SAP RAR can be used by downstream processes and applications.

It is even more important to remember that SAP RAR testing should not be used to fix issues in upstream or downstream processes which are not related to SAP RAR. For example, if a defect is opened during testing because of incomplete customer address data on a sales order, the test management team must ensure, that such item is not processed by SAP RAR implementation team, since this is not a problem with the SAP RAR implementation.

To get the best testing results and be efficient about testing, particularly when teams are located around the world, we strongly recommend test execution be conducted in one location.

When testers and project team members come together in one room, they collaborate better and solve problems faster.

During the test execution, test managers must ensure, that testers are not distracted by their daily work and instead are entirely focused on the test execution. Future SAP RAR business users should not see testing as a nuisance but as an opportunity to get hands-on experience with the new tool and understand the new end-to-end processes. The change management team should emphasize the importance and advantages of testing, particularly the fact that thorough testing will mean fewer problems in production.

As mentioned before, SAP RAR test execution must include testing based on migration data. Therefore, test managers must ensure that SAP RAR data migration testing and validation is finished before the data is handed over to the testers.

Any compromises on the testing timeline can lead to reductions in the scope of testing. If all tests are not conducted, problems can arise in production. Therefore, test managers need to include contingency plans in the testing schedule.

During SAP RAR user acceptance tests, testers may insufficiently test period-end closing scenarios or not test them at all. We strongly recommend conducting these tests because period-end closing activities in SAP RAR are the most important part of work in production. Sometimes implementation teams assume readiness for a successful period-end closing because multiple SAP RAR test cases, which cover multiple steps in SAP RAR, have been executed successfully.

Again, SAP RAR tests can only be executed successfully if most critical revenue-relevant processes in a company are tested end-to-end. Testing single processes will not help to identify problems in an integrated environment. That's why period-end closing activities have to be tested thoroughly.

4.4 Cutover activities

A "cutover" plan is a "scenario" or a "game plan" that lists out the tasks that need to be done for to go-live. In other words, the cutover plan is there to begin the new functionality or application in a productive environment. After successful execution of the cutover plan, legacy applications are not used anymore.

Typically, cutover planning includes the following activities:

- Identifying cutover tasks and resources,
- Identifying cutover execution environments,
- Sequencing cutover activities and determining dependencies,
- Estimating cutover timing,
- Establishing cutover execution schedules,
- Integrating data validation/verification procedures and resources.

We highly recommend defining a very detailed cutover plan for your SAP RAR implementation. It should include a detailed (ideally hourly) schedule of migration activities and all other activities required to set up SAP RAR production. Typically, the project implementation team is in charge of creating the cutover plan, and it's best to make sure that all affected and impacted parties are involved in making the plan. Keep in mind that the cutover plan must include both business as well as IT implementation activities.

You will also need a communication plan to be in place for cutover planning and execution. This is important for creating awareness within the organization about the changes and forgetting feedback on the planned activities and execution schedule. You should also plan to provide regular status updates during cutover execution, to ensure smooth execution of the planned activities.

It's best to start very early with the cutover plan to create a comprehensive plan and properly schedule all activities. This way the implementation team has a chance to test execution of cutover activities at an early stage and start fine-tuning the plan based on feedback received during the testing of the cutover plan.

The cutover plan should also be validated during test phases. In this way, the cutover plan will have passed different levels of validation before it is used in the productive environment. Unfortunately, not all cutover activities can be tested during integration and user acceptance testing. For example, one-time activities that take place in the productive environment, and communication to external stakeholders, as well as other administrative tasks, cannot be tested in a testing environment.

It is best practice to have support ready and waiting, in case of problems with the actual cutover in the productive environment. You also need to prepare a list of people (including their emergency contact details) on the implementation team and key contacts from all over the organization. This inner circle of people must stay informed on progress.

Conclusion/Outlook

5

Implementation of the new standard on accounting for revenue from contracts with customers is a challenge which can impact broad areas of a company.

For example, companies have to adopt the new requirements of the five-step approach that impact the timing of revenue recognition. In addition, IFRS 15 implementation might even have an impact on employee compensation models.

All these changes impact far more than the accounting and finance departments of a company.

In this book, we have described the regulatory background of IFRS 15 and the challenges associated with its implementation. IFRS 15 is applicable for all contracts with customers, except leasing contracts, insurance contracts and financial instruments. In some industries like the telecommunications and the software industries, the impact is especially high.

Implementation of IFRS 15 has to be supported by an IT solution. Usually, each substantial IT implementation impacts multiple areas of the existing IT architecture and existing processes, and the implementations are a challenge for both the business and IT sides of a company.

IFRS 15 can be implemented in parallel with SAP Revenue Accounting and Reporting, but the complex and critical task must be done the right way and at the right time. That's because internal business processes and reporting are strongly impacted. A joint IFRS 15 and SAP RAR implementation should be seen as a good opportunity to critically assess existing revenue accounting-relevant processes and fix old, inefficient and broken "business as usual" processes. This will allow companies to improve business efficiency and automation while keeping costs low for implementation as well as maintenance after go-live. Those companies that drag their feet and have to comply on a manual basis each month after January 2018 will be at a disadvantage, due to the high cost of manually reconciling accounts and creating reports.

In this book, we've described the functionalities of SAP RAR and why it can be a good choice for IFRS 15 implementation. In addition to company-specific (internal), regulatory and legal requirements, it's important to consider:

- Existing IT architecture,
- Automation for revenue accounting processes,
- Audit-related requirements.

Of course, any IT solution to support IFRS 15 implementation should fit into the existing IT landscape. Furthermore, it should support automation of the processes in revenue accounting. Over the long term, it should not cause additional manual work in the finance department. Software selected to enable revenue reporting based on the new standard should also meet audit requirements.

SAP Revenue Accounting and Reporting supports integration with SAP's own products and can also be integrated with non-SAP applications. Functionalities provided with SAP RAR enable companies to setup revenue accounting processes in accordance with IFRS 15 rules and their internal requirements, and they enable process automation.

As mentioned earlier, IFRS 15 becomes effective for all financial reporting periods starting on or after January 1, 2018. Every company affected by this change is obliged to start accounting for revenue from contracts with customers based on the new standard from that day onward.

Given the (remaining) short implementation timeline and potential challenges, companies must act quickly and effectively. You will need a team for the implementation and for change management that includes members from all affected areas. This is clearly a challenge for many companies but is a key success factor.

Abbreviations

ALV list	SAP List Viewer
ARPU	Average revenue per user
ARRE	Aptitude Revenue Recognition Engine
BOM	Bill of Material
BRFplus	Business Rule Framework plus
BW	Business Warehouse
CI	Convergent Invoicing
CFO	Chief Financial Officer
CRM	Customer Relationship Management
ERP	Enterprise resource planning
FASB	Financial Accounting Standards Board
FI	Finance
HGB	Handelsgesetzbuch (German GAAP)
IFRS	International Financial Reporting Standards
IAS	International Accounting Standard
IASB	International Accounting Standard Board
KPI	Key Performance Indicator
POB	Performance Obligation
POC	Percentage of completion
PMO	Project Management Office
RAI	Revenue Accounting Item
RAR	Revenue Accounting and Reporting
SAP SD	SAP Module for Sales & Distribution
SEC	U.S. Securities and Exchange Commission
SSP	Stand-alone selling price
TRG	Transition Resource Group
UI	User Interface
US GAAP	US Generally Accepted Accounting Principles

Author Biographies

Bajram Midzaiti

Bajram Midzaiti is a Senior Analyst with Accenture in the Finance & Enterprise Performance practice. He is specialized in SAP Financials and particularly in revenue accounting and reporting processes. Bajram is also an expert on international regulatory requirements according to IFRS 15. He supports customers in post-merger integration and has been working on implementations of the SAP revenue accounting module since 2014.

Bajram holds a diploma in economic science from the University of Duisburg-Essen with a focus on finance and management accounting. He is also certified in SAP FI.

Dr. Leo Lehr

Dr. Leo Lehr studied physics and economics and began working at Accenture in 2001, directly after graduation. Leo mostly serves clients in Communications, Media and Technology, helping them use SAP technologies to improve their businesses. During his career, Leo contributed to several books on Business Intelligence and Analytics in finance, published several Points of View (e.g. a study on Compliance in IT Outsourcing), and performed market studies for Analytics and Mobility. He has also been interviewed by CIO magazine for his expertise on HANA. Leo leads the Accenture SAP Industry Center of Excellence in the Communications, Media & Technology industry for Europe, Africa & Latin America. It is located near the SAP headquarters Walldorf.

David Gilow

David Gilow is an Accenture consultant with a focus on the Aerospace & Defense industry, as well as the Telecommunications sector. He specializes in finance projects, including IFRS 15 implementations.

Before joining Accenture, David worked for a Big 4 company in accounting advisory for the financial services sector. He holds a M.S. degree in economics from the University of York in England. David also studied in Mannheim, Germany, and in Lausanne, Switzerland.

Oleg Podlesnov

Oleg Podlesnov joined Accenture's SAP technology practice in 2011. His SAP journey started in 2004 when he got certified as an SAP Business One consultant. After working in this area, Oleg began to support large international SAP ECC rollouts and became specialized in order-to-cash and logistics processes. Since 2014, Oleg has been working on SAP Revenue Accounting and Reporting implementations as a project manager.

Oleg has a degree in business administration (Business Information Systems) from the University of Cooperative Education in Stuttgart.

Simona Fiano

Simona Fiano is a Senior Manager in Accenture's Technology Consulting practice specializing in finance. She has a strong focus on large finance transformation programs and years of experience with SAP Products (ERP, S/4 HANA, SAP-RAR, etc.).

Simona's expertise is in the telecommunications industry, where she has spent several years consulting for national and international companies.

She also serves as head of Accenture's IFRS 15 Center of Excellence for the Europe, Middle East, Africa and Latin America (EALA) regions.

Simona graduated with a degree in mathematics from the University of Naples Federico II in Italy.

Tolga Turhan

Tolga Turhan is an associate manager in Accenture's Technology Consulting practice specialized in finance, with a focus on business consolidation, S/4 HANA – Central Finance and IFRS.

Tolga has consulted for many years on national and international transformation projects, predominantly in the Aerospace & Defense industry.

Prior to joining Accenture, Tolga worked as a tax and financial advisor in Germany which gave him fundamental insights into the financial industry. He then continued his education in the US and holds a B.S in business administration and an MBA with concentrations in finance and accounting.

Vanessa Gerwens

Vanessa Gerwens is an Accenture consultant in the Finance & Enterprise Performance practice with a strong focus on S/4 HANA Finance Implementation and Project Management. Over the years, she has honed her skills in post-merger integrations and has a strong focus on data migration and SOX audits. Starting in February 2017, Vanessa began supporting a large S/4HANA Finance implementation project from a Core Finance perspective. During the past five years, Vanessa has also gained experience in the Communication, Media & Technology Industry.

Vanessa studied at the University of Heidelberg, earning a master's degree in politics and history with a regional focus on South Asia.

Markus Lüttenberg

Markus Lüttenberg joined Accenture in May 2016 as an intern and continued working as a trainee during his studies. Markus earned a B.S. in business economics from the Frankfurt School of Finance & Management and has done an apprenticeship in the banking sector. In early 2017, he was pursuing a M.S. in management at the University of Mannheim.

CPSIA information can be obtained
at www.ICGtesting.com
Printed in the USA
BVOW05*1420080118
504716BV00017B/431/P

9 783981 883701